CHATEAU STE. MICHELLE

STAR-SPANGLED
COOKING
A FOOD LOVER'S TOUR OF AMERICA

FOUNDING
SPONSOR

LIBERTY
1886·1986

Copyright © 1987 Chateau Ste. Michelle
One Stimson Lane
Woodinville, Washington 98072

Produced by Stewart, Tabori & Chang, Inc.
740 Broadway
New York, New York 10003

Library of Congress Cataloging-in-Publication Data

Star-spangled cooking.

  Includes index.
  1. Cookery, American.   I. Stewart, Tabori & Chang.
TX715.S7849 1987   641.5973   87-1914
ISBN 1-55670-015-6

Editor: Bob Betz
Design Director: Ted Baseler

Text:
  John Doerper:
  The Northwest

  Paul Gregutt:
  New England
  The Mid-Atlantic
  The South

Joanne Will:
  The Midwest
Recipes:
  Karen Johnson LaFlamme
  Christy Nordstrom
  John Doerper—The Northwest

Food Photography:
  Matthew Klein
Food Stylist:
  Andrea Swenson
Prop Stylist:
  Linda Cheverton
Special thanks to:
  Allen Shoup
  Leslie Stoker
  Jeff Batzli
  Mary Cregan
  Kathy Rosenbloom
  John Sturman

DEDICATION

In 1983, Chateau Ste. Michelle became a Founding Sponsor of the Statue of Liberty/Ellis Island Foundation, pledging our efforts to raise funds for the restoration of two of the country's greatest monuments. Thanks to the public's generosity, by 1986 the statue had been restored to its original splendor. The nation celebrated by giving itself the most festive birthday party in its history.

Now it's Ellis Island's turn. With a target date of 1992, this historic immigration station will be restored and given back to America as a living memorial to our international roots—just in time for Ellis Island's 100th birthday.

America is a country of immigrants. More than any other modern nation, the United States represents a sort of ethnic synergy, where old cultural boundaries blur and break and something new is born. Nowhere, perhaps, is this process more exciting than in the dynamic evolution of American regional cooking.

No longer held by the deep cement of the traditions of their native lands, immigrants were free to experiment with the unfamiliar foods they found in their new home. The land was abundant. Inspiration prevailed—in the red heat of Southwest chiles, the dark mystery of Minnesota wild rice, the buttery flesh of New England lobster. The natural opulence of the earth and sea gave each region its own culinary personality.

Chateau Ste. Michelle shares this blessing of abundance. For more than fifty years we have pioneered grape growing and wine making in Washington's Columbia Valley. Its unique soil, climate, and geographic location make the valley one of the world's few great regions for growing classic European grape types. Like the Ellis Island immigrants, all our grapes originally came from Europe. And, like those early pioneers, they found a willing home in the new land. Over the decades, our internationally acclaimed wines have demonstrated the exciting potential of cultivating old-world traditions in a new-world environment.

By making the most of the rich variety of their native pantry, Americans have developed a cuisine of unlimited gustatory satisfaction and created a whole nation of food and wine lovers. We dedicate this book to American cooks, and to all of us who love and cherish good food and drink.

In the heart of Washington's vineyards, Chateau Ste. Michelle's River Ridge winery overlooks the Columbia River.

PREFACE

When European immigrants passed through Ellis Island, they brought with them the culinary secrets of their homelands. Once they settled—whether on the shores of the Great Lakes or in the backwoods of Virginia—their old recipes found new interpretations, and new foods were adapted to old traditions. Thus a local cuisine began to develop, and this process will never be finished; regional cooking is a living thing, responding endlessly to the creativity of its inventors and the productivity of its natural environment.

From the early Spanish explorers to the twentieth-century Vietnamese, each wave of immigrants has marveled at the richness of America's natural bounty. The variety of the landscape is stunning—islands, valleys, mountains, plains, deltas, seacoasts, basins, and ranges—and the country boasts a smorgasbord of climates, water temperatures, and altitudes. All this diversity brings forth culinary ingredients distinct to each region. Avocados abound in California, not in Maine. Johannisberg Riesling grapes flourish in Washington State vineyards, not in Louisiana. Variety is the foundation of each region's cooking.

Chateau Ste. Michelle offers this book to celebrate the marriage of land and human imagination, and the delicious results of that union. We have divided America into eight regions, according more to cultural differences than to hard-and-fast borderlines. We explore the specific effects that each region's natural abundance has had—and still has—on its inhabitants.

The recipes in this book were developed at various points in American history. Some, like Southern fried chicken, are tradition-bound, rooted in the nation's older, more mature cuisines. Others are very recent, such as California's unusual pizza with sun-dried tomatoes and goat cheese. Our idea is to chart a culinary map so that the reader may fully appreciate both the gastronomic and the historic joys of a journey across the country in search of new flavors, personal roots, or long-forgotten favorite dishes.

We invite you to join us on a food lover's tour, with this working cookbook as your guide. And we hope you will become part of the dynamic process yourself, inventing and adapting and playing your own role in the ever-changing face of American cuisine.

The French Empire-style Chateau Ste.
Michelle is surrounded by eighty-seven
acres of arboretum-like grounds.

CONTENTS

THE NORTHWEST

RECIPES

The Pacific Northwest, in many respects, represents a microcosm of the entire country: the land rises from the Pacific Ocean in surf-tossed cliffs and sheltered bays, extends across low coastal mountains to fertile valleys and high alpine mountains and on to inland plateaus where prairies and wheat fields stretch to the horizon.

The region runs the gamut of landscapes—rain forests and deserts, glaciated mountains and verdant fields. Its spine is the Cascade Range, which runs from British Columbia south to California. The Cascades divide the region into a superficially "wet" west side and a "dry" east side. Yet the west is brighter than its gloomy reputation suggests, and the east never swelters like the arid Southwest. The climate of the Pacific Northwest belies its northern latitude; it is surprisingly mild, due mostly to the warm Japan Current just offshore. Winters are just frosty enough to vernalize fruit trees and shrubs successfully, while the summer sun creates growing seasons long enough to ripen a full array of the earth's produce.

One can hardly wonder that a region of such geographic and climatic diversity produces a variety of exceptionally flavorful foods, from fruits, nuts, and vegetables to fish and shellfish to meats and cheeses. In the past few decades the Pacific Northwest has even emerged as a world-class producer of classic wines.

The Northwest isn't so much home to a specific culinary style, as Louisiana is to Cajun or the Southwest is to Tex Mex, as much as it offers an abundance of raw ingredients. Its inland and coastal waters teem with shellfish: oysters of myriad sizes and shapes, Dun-geness crab, crayfish, luscious pink scallops, mussels, shrimp, clams, and the elongated geoduck. Its selection of fish also offers an embarrassment of riches. Red, pink, and silver salmon, sturgeon, rockfish, sablefish, and cod are pulled from the waters by the tons, supporting one of the nation's foremost fishing fleets. Smoked or dried, rolled into sushi or sashimi, grilled or poached, made into chowder, bisques, or mousses, these gifts of the sea are the foundation of many Northwestern meals.

PRECEDING OVERLEAF: Majestic mountains dominate the fogbound landscape of the Washington coast.

ABOVE: A wildflower blazes with color in Washington's Yakima Valley, where cherries, grapes, asparagus, and other fruits and vegetables grow in profusion.

There is a wide choice of meats, too. The broad valleys on both sides of the Cascades boast numerous breeds of beef cattle, milk-fed kid, veal, and lamb. The forests, fields, and marshes host chucker, pheasant, Canada geese, partridge, quail, and duck fattened on yellow corn, while the mountains are home to herds of white-tail deer, moose, elk, mountain lion, and bear.

Wild greens, enhanced with the colorful tang of flowers, add a distinctive note to Northwestern salads. Herb farms dot the landscape bringing the full array of fresh herbs to market and the restaurant table. Nasturtium flowers, arugula, lamb's-quarters, radicchio, and the like are available year-round.

Without its own distinct, definable regional style, the Pacific Northwest has adapted to assume an international flavor. Recipes based on those of other countries or regions here take on new dimensions, the exceptional freshness and high quality of the local ingredients demanding a unique treatment. Just as the Northwest's landscape represents a microcosm, so, too, does its cookery. A new pride in its produce pervades the region. One finds an appreciation and demand for Cascade huckleberries and Sauvie Island beans, Wenatchee apricots and Okanogan apples, Hood River and Rogue River pears, Yakima cherries and peppers, Skagit Valley cauliflower, mussels, and Dungeness crab. And this natural profusion has created a hands-on approach to food.

In recent years, innovative restaurant chefs have combined the region's most exciting ingredients into a peerless cuisine, making the Pacific Northwest a culinary mecca. The emerging symbiosis between produce and chefs impels both toward ever-higher standards.

Kevin McKenzie, owner-chef of Rover's Restaurant in Seattle, moved north from California because there is less distance from producer to market in the Northwest. Not only does he love the ready availability of first-rate fresh produce, but he enjoys dealing directly with the people who catch and grow it. McKenzie has "a country restaurant in the city." Tony Kischner of the Shoalwater Restaurant in Seaview moved from Seattle

LEFT: Clamming on the Oregon coast. The waters of the Pacific Northwest offer up a staggering array of shellfish.
RIGHT: A hops field in the Yakima Valley.

to the coast simply to be closer to the oysters and fish of Willapa Bay and the lower Columbia River. He scouts daily for the freshest of the buttery Columbia River chinook salmon and for the freshest sturgeon, bottom-fish, and razor clams. Will Masset's Birchfield Manor opened in the heart of the Yakima Valley, minutes from the source of tangy greens, berry orchards, and hoofed cattle.

Local pride doesn't focus on one season or ingredient, and the year-long abundance of the Northwest could pique the envy of the most fastidious French gourmet. Spring is signaled by the arrival of flavorful Walla Walla and Yakima Valley asparagus (white stalk and all), delicately bitter dandelion greens, crunchy fiddleheads, sweet sugar peas, the first salmon of the year, and the pungent morel mushroom.

Summer brings herbs and vegetables (both the exotic and the mundane), geoduck clams and squash, fresh halibut and tangy cucumbers, fresh local shrimp and artichokes, broccoli, cauliflower, Walla Walla sweet onions, and aromatic flowers for salads. Summer is also

salmon-barbecue time in the Northwest. This king of local waters is the focus of festivals and backyard meals from Southern Oregon to the Canadian border.

Delightful among the fruits of summer are sweet strawberries, red and golden cherries, wild blackberries and huckleberries, raspberries, apricots, and blueberries. Gravensteins mark the beginning of apple harvest, while sweet nectarines, peaches, Pasco cantaloupes, and Hermiston watermelons peak during the warm days of August.

In fall the fragrant rare Comice pears from Oregon's Rogue River Valley are a perfect accompaniment to the nationally renowned Oregon blue cheese. Lamb from the San Juan Islands is prepared with fresh local chanterelles, the sweet mushrooms' aroma permeating the kitchen. Locals eat their fill of oysters at numerous shucking championships in coastal towns or indulge in homemade sausages, sauerkraut, kraut ranzas, and pickles at the annual fall fest in Odessa, Washington. To quench the thirsty, gallons of fresh apple cider flow from roadside stands.

LEFT: Piles of lumber stand on a Seattle dock. The vast forests of the Pacific Northwest make it one of the nation's biggest timber-producing regions.

RIGHT: Neat rows of crabs on display at the Seattle Pike Place market, home to a vast collection of the state's abundance.

The cold waters of winter produce succulent rock-fish, ling cod, and Puget Sound Dungeness crab (smaller but more flavorful than its coastal cousins) for seafood markets and restaurants. Once again, buttery bivalves—oysters, meaty clams, and mussels—are ubiquitous. With luck, the undaunted eater will search out one of the Northwest's simplest treats: just-shuck-ed Olympia oysters topped with fresh, nutty sturgeon caviar, accompanied by a dry Northwest semillon, sauvignon blanc, or even a crisp sparkling wine.

Great herds of dairy cattle dot the Pacific Northwest. They graze on green grasses, yielding copious quantities of milk and sweet cream. The regional cheeses are of uniquely refined flavor and quality. Besides the renowned Oregon blue, there is the equally famous golden Cheddar from Tillamook. But superb Cheddar is also made in Bandon on the southern Oregon coast, in Olympia at the head of Puget Sound, and by Washington Cheese in Mount Vernon.

A creamy Brie—made by the Blue Heron Cheese

Irrigated wheat fields near Ephrata, Washington. The Pacific Northwest is one of the nation's breadbaskets.

Company—also hails from Tillamook. Northwesterners are long-time fans of the peculiar but tasty Cougar Gold, the firm nutty Cheddar made by the Washington State University creamery in Pullman. A buttery Dutch-style Gouda from Pleasant Valley Dairy in Ferndale competes with a heartier, saltier version from the Yakima Valley for the best of its type in the region.

But the Northwest's most interesting cheeses are crafted from goat's milk. Unlike the soft, mild chèvres of California and France, these tend to be firm, full of gutsy flavor, and wonderfully tangy when aged. They help to make the Pacific Northwest one of America's richest culinary treasure-troves—not just a microcosm, but a sampling of the very best the nation has to offer.

A lonely, misty stretch of the Oregon coast.

OYSTERS ON THE HALF SHELL

Recommended Wine: Sparkling Wine

2 SERVINGS

1   small piece of mild or medium-hot green
    or red chile (about ¼ × ½-inch)
½   small ripe tomato, peeled and seeded
2   or 3 shallots
2   sprigs cilantro
½   teaspoon rice vinegar

2   to 4 lemons
2   dozen very fresh oysters in the shell,
    washed
2   teaspoons natural whitefish caviar,
    optional
    Crushed ice, for serving

*Coastal residents of the Northwest down oysters by the dozen at shucking contests, but you can serve
these shellfish as Oysters on the Half Shell, an elegant appetizer.*

Make salsa: Chop chile, tomato, shallots, and cilantro. Turn into small bowl and moisten with rice vinegar; set aside.

Cut 24 very thin lemon slices on the bias (to make slices as large as possible). Carefully shuck oysters, reserving all liquor. Slip a lemon slice under each oyster and top with a tiny dab of salsa and a dab of whitefish caviar. Set oysters on crushed ice and serve.

FRIED OYSTERS

Recommended Wine: Chardonnay

2 TO 4 SERVINGS

2   dozen freshly shucked oysters, rinsed
        and drained, about ½ pint
½   teaspoon salt
½   cup all-purpose flour
½   teaspoon freshly ground white pepper
3   eggs
    Almond oil or vegetable oil for frying

Place oysters in a colander and sprinkle with salt. Set aside to drain until the surface is dry, about 10 minutes.

In shallow plate, mix flour and pepper. In shallow bowl, lightly beat eggs. Roll oysters in flour/pepper mixture, coating lightly, then drop into eggs to coat. In deep skillet, heat enough oil to measure ¼ inch deep. Fry oysters, in batches, over medium-high heat. Do not overcook; they are done as soon as the coating turns golden.

PINK SCALLOPS IN THE SHELL

Recommended Wine: Sauvignon Blanc

2 TO 4 SERVINGS

2   tablespoons unsalted butter
2   tablespoons dry white wine
1   sprig fresh chervil
    Dash of cayenne pepper
    Salt and pepper to taste
2   dozen fresh scallops in the shell (buy
        only scallops with firmly closed shells)

In deep saucepan, melt butter over medium heat. Add wine, chervil, cayenne, salt and pepper and bring to a rolling boil. Add scallops, cover and cook for 1 minute, until scallops open.

Spoon scallops, in their shells, into small bowls and pour pan juices over. Accompany with freshly baked bread and chilled white wine.

Oysters on the Half Shell.

WHITE WINE STEAMED CLAMS

Recommended Wine: Semillon

4 TO 6 SERVINGS

4   to 6 dozen littleneck clams, well
      scrubbed
     About 1 cup very dry white wine
2   tablespoons chopped cilantro or fresh
      parsley
2   tablespoons fresh lemon juice
     Freshly ground white pepper to taste
     Lemon wedges, for serving

In stainless steel or enamel pot large enough to accommodate clams in one or two layers, pour enough wine to measure about ½ inch. Add cilantro, lemon juice and pepper and bring to a boil over high heat. Add clams. Cover tightly and steam until clams open; remove at once.

Strain cooking juices through a double layer of cheesecloth and serve in cups, alongside the clams. Accompany with lemon wedges.

SHELBURNE INN CLAM FRITTERS

Recommended Wine: Fumé Blanc

6 SERVINGS

4   cups parboiled, grated potatoes
1   medium yellow onion, chopped
1   small red onion, chopped
6   to 8 fresh razor clams, chopped
6   eggs, beaten
½   cup all-purpose flour
1   tablespoon finely chopped fresh thyme
2   tablespoons finely chopped fresh oregano
3   tablespoons chopped fresh chives
⅛   teaspoon cayenne pepper
     Salt to taste
½   cup unsalted butter, melted plus
      additional butter as needed for frying

In large bowl, combine potatoes, onions, clams, eggs, flour, thyme, oregano, chives, cayenne, salt and melted butter. Mix well.

In large skillet, melt 1 tablespoon butter over medium heat. Working in batches, drop clam mixture by large spoonfuls into butter and fry for 3 to 4 minutes on each side, until golden brown. Serve hot.

NOTE: This recipe is from David Campiche, proprietor of the renowned Shelburne Inn on Washington's Long Beach Peninsula.

NORTHWEST SEAFOOD STEW

Recommended Wine: Chardonnay

6 TO 8 SERVINGS

4   tablespoons unsalted butter
2   medium onions, finely chopped
2   leeks, white part only, well washed and finely chopped
1½ pounds assorted seafood (fish chunks, whole small fish, shrimp, sea cucumber, barnacles or others)
4   to 6 cups mild chicken stock
    Salt and freshly ground black pepper to taste
1   pound crab meat or 1½ pounds tiny crabs in the shell, well-scrubbed
1   tablespoon nuoc mam (fish sauce)
1   tablespoon fresh lemon juice
1   to 2 tablespoons natural salmon or whitefish caviar
    Dash of cayenne pepper
¼   cup thinly sliced fresh chives

In heavy nonreactive stockpot, melt butter over medium-low heat. Add onions and leeks and sauté until limp, about 5 minutes.

Add seafood and sauté over medium heat, without browning, for 5 minutes.

Add enough stock to cover seafood; season with salt and pepper. Bring to a simmer. Add crab meat and stir well. Season with *nuoc mam* and lemon juice.

Carefully stir caviar into stew and then with more stock if necessary. Simmer gently for about 10 minutes; season with cayenne.

Ladle stew into individual bowls and sprinkle with chives.

NORTHWEST CHANTERELLE SAUTE

4 TO 6 SERVINGS

1   tablespoon walnut oil
1   pound fresh chanterelles or commercial mushrooms
¾   teaspoon minced garlic
1   sprig fresh rosemary
½   cup Madeira wine

In large skillet, heat walnut oil over medium-high heat until very hot. Add mushrooms and sauté briefly, about 2 minutes. Add garlic and rosemary and sauté for 2 to 3 minutes.

Add wine, cook for 30 seconds and ignite. Cook, shaking the pan until the flames subside. Cover and steam until mushrooms are tender, about 5 minutes.

NOTE: Martin Hahn at the Black Swan Cafe in LaConner, Washington, created this preparation for chanterelles collected in the local woods.

GREEN BEANS COOKED WITH SUMMER SAVORY

4 TO 6 SERVINGS

1¾ pounds fresh green beans, scarlet runner
      beans, French beans, or yellow wax
      beans
1½ ounces pork fatback, diced
1   small onion, finely chopped
1   sprig of summer savory
      Salt to taste
1   to 2 teaspoons cornstarch
1   tablespoon chopped fresh parsley

String, wash and chop or break beans.
  In large skillet, render fatback until pale golden, about 5 minutes. Add beans, onion and savory and toss until heated through, 2 to 3 minutes. Add ½ cup water and cook over low heat until crisp-tender, 5 to 8 minutes.

  Season beans with salt. Stir cornstarch into 1 tablespoon cold water and add to thicken cooking liquid. Cook for 2 to 3 minutes.

  Sprinkle beans with parsley and serve.

FRIED FENNEL

4 SERVINGS

3   fennel bulbs
1   egg
1¼ cups ice water
1⅔ cups all-purpose flour or tempura flour
      Vegetable oil for deep-frying

Cut off tops of fennel bulbs and trim. Cut bulbs lengthwise into ⅜-inch-thick slices. Wash thoroughly in several changes of cold water; drain and pat dry.

  In chilled bowl, mix egg and ice water. Sift flour and add to egg mixture. Mix together, but do not overmix; the batter should be lumpy and a powdery ring of flour should remain around the sides of the mixing bowl.

  In wok or deep-fryer, add oil to a depth of 2 inches and heat to 340 degrees. Pat fennel with paper towels to dry completely. Dip fennel pieces into batter and fry until batter is deep golden, 2 to 3 minutes.

BRUSSELS SPROUTS IN HAZELNUT BUTTER

6 SERVINGS

1   *pound Brussels sprouts, of as even a*
     size as possible, trimmed
2   *tablespoons unsalted butter*
1   *large shallot, finely chopped*
¼   *cup finely crushed toasted hazelnuts*
     Salt and freshly ground pepper to taste
1   *to 2 pinches freshly grated nutmeg*

Bring water to boil in bottom of steamer. Make a ¼-inch-deep "X" in stem ends of sprouts. Place sprouts in steamer and set over boiling water. Cover and steam until sprouts are fork-tender, 3 to 5 minutes. Immediately remove sprouts from steam.

In large saucepan, melt butter over medium heat until it begins to foam lightly. Add shallot and cook until golden, about 2 minutes. Add hazelnuts and stir. Add Brussels sprouts and toss to coat. Season with salt and pepper and a pinch or two of nutmeg. Remove from pan and serve hot.

Brussels Sprouts in Hazelnut Butter are the perfect accompaniment to a crown roast.

GRILLED STEAK WITH MOREL SAUCE

Recommended Wine: Merlot

6 SERVINGS

6   beef steaks, with or without bone
2   tablespoons olive oil
1   bottle merlot
1   small onion, minced
1   tablespoon all-purpose flour
½   cup beef broth
½   teaspoon fresh thyme
4   cloves garlic, peeled but left whole
1   bay leaf
12 pearl or small white onions
1   to 2 cups fresh morels
    Salt and freshly ground pepper

Prepare a fire in a gas or charcoal grill until the coals are ash-covered.

In a heavy skillet, quickly brown steaks in olive oil over medium heat. Remove and place on barbecue grill to cook to desired doneness over hot coals. Baste steaks with some of the wine while they cook.

Meanwhile, add onion to skillet and cook until golden and tender, about 2 minutes. Sprinkle on flour and cook, stirring, for 3 minutes. Add ½ cup wine, broth, thyme, garlic, bay leaf, pearl onions and mushrooms. Bring to a boil, reduce heat to low and simmer until beef is cooked to taste. When beef is tender, season with salt and pepper to taste and place on individual serving plates. Spoon some sauce over each and accompany with grilled vegetables.

The wild morel mushrooms grown in the Pacific Northwest give this Grilled Steak a unique regional flavor.

STIR-FRIED CUCUMBER WITH PORK

Recommended Wine: Gewürztraminer
6 SERVINGS

¼   *pound boneless pork butt*
1   *tablespoon thin soy sauce*
1   *tablespoon dry sherry or Shaoxing wine*
1   *large seedless cucumber*
    Salt to taste
2   *tablespoons vegetable oil*
2   *large cloves garlic, minced*
½   *cup unsalted chicken stock*
    Steamed white rice, for serving

Cut pork butt across grain into ¼-inch-thick slices; cut slices into narrow ¼ × 2-inch strips.

In small bowl, combine soy sauce and sherry. Add pork and set aside to marinate for 15 minutes.

Halve cucumber lengthwise and cut into ¼ × ¼ × 2-inch strips. Sprinkle with salt; set aside for 15 minutes.

Heat 1 tablespoon oil in wok or heavy skillet. Drain pork; reserve liquid.

When oil begins to smoke, add pork and stir-fry for about 1 minute. Remove pork from pan; carefully rinse pan under running water.

Add remaining 1 tablespoon oil to the wok or skillet. Squeeze cucumber dry in paper towels. When oil just begins to smoke, add cucumber and stir-fry until strips are heated through, about 30 seconds. Add pork and garlic, stir briefly and add stock. Bring mixture to a boil, remove pork and cucumber to serving bowl with slotted spoon and set aside; keep warm.

Increase heat under wok to very high and reduce stock to the consistency of a gravy, 2 to 3 minutes. Pour over pork and cucumber and toss to coat well. Serve with steamed rice.

OREGON BLUE CHEESE BURGERS

Recommended Wine: Pinot Noir
4 SERVINGS

1½ *pounds ground beef*
    Salt and freshly ground pepper to taste
3   *tablespoons cream cheese, at room*
        temperature
1   *tablespoon crumbled Oregon blue cheese,*
        at room temperature
1   *medium onion, minced*
1   *teaspoon prepared horseradish*

Prepare a fire in a gas or charcoal grill until coals are ash-covered.

Meanwhile, sprinkle ground beef

with salt and pepper; mix lightly but thoroughly. Divide meat into 8 equal portions and shape into 4-inch patties.

In small bowl, combine cream cheese, blue cheese, onion, and horse-radish. Place 1 tablespoon of mixture on each of 4 patties. Top each with remaining patties. Press edges to-gether securely to seal.

Grill burgers 5 to 6 inches above coals for 5 to 6 minutes on one side; turn and grill for 5 to 6 minutes, or to desired doneness.

CHICKEN WITH RIESLING AND APPLES

Recommended Wine: Johannisberg Riesling

4 TO 6 SERVINGS

5	tablespoons unsalted butter
4	tart apples, peeled and thinly sliced
1	tablespoon sugar
1	tablespoon candied ginger, sliced
3	tablespoons Calvados or applejack
¾	cup dry riesling
8	whole, boneless, skinless chicken breasts
	Salt and freshly ground pepper
1	tablespoon vegetable oil
2	shallots, diced
½	cup rich chicken stock
1	pint heavy cream

In large skillet, melt 2 tablespoons butter over medium-low heat. Add apples in single layer, sprinkle with sugar and add candied ginger. Sauté, turning, until slightly browned, 3 to 4 minutes.

In small saucepan, warm the Cal-vados over low heat. Carefully pour over apples and ignite, shaking the pan until the flames subside.

Add wine and cook until apples are tender, about 5 minutes. Set aside.

Season chicken breasts with salt and pepper. In large skillet, melt remain-ing 3 tablespoons butter with oil over medium heat. Add chicken and brown on both sides. Set aside.

Let skillet cool to medium. Add shallots and sauté for 2 minutes. Return chicken to skillet, cover par-tially and cook until just done, about 5 minutes. Set aside and keep warm.

Discard fat in skillet and add broth. Cook over medium-high heat, scrap-ing up brown bits that cling to bottom of skillet. Add cream and reduce heat to low. Gently simmer broth and cream until thickened, about 5 minutes.

Add sautéed apples and cook briefly, just to heat through. Serve with roast potatoes and steamed vegetables.

SALMON IN OREGON HAZELNUT BUTTER

Recommended Wine: Johannisberg Riesling

6 SERVINGS

3   tablespoons unsalted butter
6   7-ounce salmon fillets (preferably
     chinook)
     Salt and freshly ground pepper to taste
1½ cups fish stock
1½ tablespoons fresh lemon juice
½   cup Hazelnut Butter (recipe follows)

Preheat oven to 500 degrees.

Select a jelly roll or roasting pan large enough to hold the fillets and deep enough to hold liquid. Coat pan generously using all of butter.

Lightly season salmon fillets with salt and pepper. Lay them in prepared pan and pour fish stock and lemon juice over. Place 1 tablespoon Hazelnut Butter on top of each fillet.

Bake salmon for 10 minutes. Remove to warmed serving plates.

Pour salmon cooking liquid into medium sauté pan and bring to a boil over high heat. Add remaining 2 tablespoons Hazelnut Butter and simmer until thickened, 3 to 5 minutes.

Divide sauce among fillets and serve immediately.

NOTE: This recipe comes from Tony Kischner of the Shoalwater Restaurant in Seaview, Washington.

HAZELNUT BUTTER

MAKES 1 CUP

½   cup unsalted butter, softened
⅓   cup ground roasted hazelnuts
1   shallot, minced
1   teaspoon minced garlic
1   tablespoon fresh parsley, minced

Combine all ingredients in small mixing bowl until well blended. Set aside at room temperature until needed or cover and refrigerate if making in advance.

If the Pacific Northwest is renowned for one fish, it is salmon; here a simple interpretation with Oregon Hazelnut Butter.

SESAME FLOUNDER

Recommended Wine: Chenin Blanc

4 TO 6 SERVINGS

1   *pound flounder filets, skinned*
2   *tablespoons dry sherry or Shaoxing wine*
¼   *teaspoon salt*
2   *green onions cut on the bias into ½-inch*
     sections
     Pinch of freshly ground black pepper
¼   *cup cornstarch*
¼   *cup all-purpose flour*
1   *egg, beaten*
3   *tablespoons ice water*
½   *cup sesame seeds, lightly toasted*
2   *cups almond oil or vegetable oil for*
     deep-frying

Cut flounder fillets into bite-size pieces. In shallow bowl, mix the sherry, salt, and green onions. Add fish, refrigerate and marinate, stirring occasionally, for 10 minutes.

Drain fish pieces; refrigerate to chill well before frying.

In small bowl, sift cornstarch with flour. Add egg and ice water and mix well. Spread out sesame seeds on shallow plate.

In large wok, heat oil over medium heat to 375 degrees. Dip fish chunks first into batter, and then coat on all sides with sesame seeds. Deep-fry 3 to 4 pieces at a time, turning once, until crisp and golden brown, 2 to 3 minutes.

Serve fish hot, with rice, stir-fried vegetables and tsunemono pickles.

HALIBUT IN ANISE CHEESE SAUCE

Recommended Wine: Fumé Blanc

4 SERVINGS

4   *halibut steaks, ¼ to ½ pound each*
     Salt and freshly ground white pepper to
     taste
     Juice of ½ lemon and ½ lime, mixed
1   *cup cooked small shrimp, at room*
     temperature
     Anise Cheese Sauce (recipe follows)

Season halibut steaks with salt and pepper. Using a small basting brush, brush halibut with citrus juice on both sides. Place steaks in top part of steamer, set steamer unit over vigorously boiling water. Cover tightly. Steam until done, 10 to 15 minutes per pound.

Place steaks on serving platter, decorate with shrimp and pour sauce over. Serve hot.

ANISE CHEESE SAUCE

MAKES 2 CUPS

About 1 cup halibut skin and bones
2   cups cold water
1   small carrot, cut into thirds
½   small onion
1   sprig of fennel
1   bay leaf
6   black peppercorns
2   tablespoons unsalted butter
2   tablespoons all-purpose flour
½   cup heavy cream
2   egg yolks, at room temperature
     Salt and freshly ground pepper to taste
     Pinch of cayenne pepper
¼   cup grated anise-flavored cheese

In nonreactive medium saucepan, combine fish skin and bones, water, carrot, onion, fennel, bay leaf, and peppercorns. Cook, uncovered, over high heat for 5 minutes. Skim off scum that rises to the surface. Reduce heat and cook, covered, over medium heat for 25 minutes. Strain; there should be 1 cup of stock

In heavy skillet, melt butter over medium-low heat. Stir in flour and cook, stirring, for 2 to 3 minutes to make a roux. Add fish stock and stir in cream. Bring just to a boil and remove from heat.

Carefully stir in egg yolks. Season with salt, pepper and cayenne. Stir in cheese until smooth. Serve immediately over halibut.

PASTA WITH SALMON

Recommended Wine: Chardonnay

2 SERVINGS

8   dried cloud ear mushrooms
2   tablespoons vegetable oil
2   thin slices fresh ginger root, peeled
1   clove garlic, sliced
2   salmon steaks, each cut 1½ inches thick
3   cups unsalted chicken stock
1   tablespoon dry sherry or Shaoxing wine
     Salt and freshly ground white pepper to taste
1   teaspoon (sweet) red Chinese vinegar or sweetened red wine vinegar
4   drops sesame oil
2   to 3 cups cooked pasta, (conchiglie, tortiglioni, farfalle, capelletti, spiedini, ruote or other small variety)
2   sprigs of cilantro, for garnish
2   teaspoons salmon caviar, drained, for garnish

In small bowl, soak cloud ear mushrooms in warm water to cover by 2 inches for 30 minutes, or until softened.

In large wok, heat oil over medium

heat until hot. Add ginger and garlic and cook until nut-brown in color; remove. (Do not burn garlic. If it blackens, start over with fresh oil.)

Add 1 salmon steak to wok and sauté until opaque. Remove from wok and keep warm. Sauté remaining steak.

In a flameproof clay pot, combine chicken stock, mushrooms, sherry, salt and pepper. Bring to a boil over high heat; reduce heat to low.

Carefully add salmon steaks, taking care that they do not break apart. Cover and simmer gently for 5 to 7 minutes, until salmon is cooked through.

Uncover and carefully stir in red vinegar and sesame oil.

To serve, make a ring of pasta on each plate and place salmon steak in center. If sauce is thin, reduce over high heat. Pour sauce over pasta and salmon. Garnish with cilantro and salmon caviar.

FRESH CRAB MEAT WITH FENNEL

Recommended Wine: Gewürztraminer

6 SERVINGS

2	tablespoons vegetable oil
1	clove garlic, chopped
2	shallots, chopped
6	ounces fresh crab meat
1/3	cup julienne-cut daikon
1	carrot, peeled and cut into julienne
1/2	cup julienne-cut fennel bulb (finocchio)
1/2	bunch green onions (green part only), cut lengthwise into thin strips
2	teaspoons nuoc mam fish sauce
1/2	teaspoon freshly ground pepper

In a large skillet, heat oil over high heat. Add garlic and shallots and sauté, stirring constantly, until golden brown.

Add crab meat and stir-fry until browned. Add julienned vegetables and stir-fry for 1 minute to heat through. Stir in fish sauce and pepper and serve immediately, with steamed rice.

Quick stir-frying is the secret to preparing Fresh Crab Meat with Fennel.

Poached Spiced Pears evoke the best from Washington's orchards.

BIRCHFIELD MANOR GORGONZOLA APRICOTS

6 SERVINGS

4   ounces Gorgonzola cheese, crumbled and
      at room temperature
8   ounces cream cheese, at room
      temperature
      Salt and freshly ground white pepper to
      taste
½   teaspoon Worcestershire sauce
      Few drops of Tabasco sauce
¼   teaspoon Maggi seasoning
6   apricots, halved and pitted

In mixing bowl, mash Gorgonzola into a paste. Add cream cheese, a little at a time, and blend until smooth. Season with salt, pepper, Worcestershire, Tabasco and Maggi seasoning.

To serve, spoon cheese mixture into a pastry bag and pipe into apricot halves.

POACHED SPICED PEARS

Recommended Wine: Late Harvest White Riesling

6 SERVINGS

6   large firm Anjou or Bosc pears
2   tablespoons fresh lemon juice
12   to 24 whole cloves
4   cups rich late harvest riesling wine
      Fresh lime juice, optional

Remove blossom ends and stems from large pears. Peel. Cut in half lengthwise and remove center cores with melon baller. Rub with lemon juice. Stick 1 clove into each pear half.

In large enamel or stainless steel skillet, bring wine to a boil over high heat. Boil until reduced by half. Add pears, reduce heat to very low, and simmer for 10 to 15 minutes, or until just soft. Adjust acid level with lime juice if syrup is too sweet.

Let pears cool in wine. Remove cloves. Serve at room temperature or chilled, topped with some of the poaching syrup.

THE
DEEP SOUTH

RECIPES

Green Turtle Soup

Louisiana Filé Gumbo

Hush Puppies

Corn-Chutney Muffins

Johnny Cake

Corn, Okra and Tomatoes

Stir-Fried Mixed Greens

Delta Rice

Red Beans

Shirred Eggs with Jarlsberg Grits

Duck and Eggplant Jambalaya

Rabbit Dijon with Leeks and Wild Mushrooms

Bayou Chicken

Dry Marinated Spare Ribs

Bread Pudding with Apricot-Fig Whiskey Compote

Pecan Pie with Nutty Pastry

Cashaw Pie

When the taste changes with every bite and the last bite is as good as the first, that's Cajun!"

The person who spoke those words is a little prejudiced, because he happens to be Cajun. He is Paul Prudhomme, the chef who put Louisiana cooking on the map and made us all suddenly aware of spicy red gumbo, honey-rich pralines, tangy crawfish etouffé, and shrimp-laden jambalayas, Through these dishes, ingredients like gumbo filé, roux, okra, cayenne, and andouille sausage have worked their way into the culinary language of the nation and have transcended Louisiana to become representative of the Deep South.

"It is no exaggeration to say that the finest and most definitive regional cooking in America is that of Louisiana," says Craig Claiborne. "That cooking, generally known as Cajun and Creole, is by far the widest in scope and broadest in taste."

As this colorful, excitingly rich food blends into the American mainstream, it shouts tales about its ancestral roots. For it has become associated with the Deep South in a way no other style of cooking has, despite all the hush puppies, grits, and Southern fried chicken you can find there. And it is anything but new.

"Cajun cuisine is a recipe in itself," wrote Marie-Louise Comeaux Manual, former director of Home Economics at the University of Southwestern Louisiana. "For ingredients take the classical French cuisine, combine it with Spanish classical cuisine, blend well, take herbs and spices from France and Spain and sometimes couple with seasoning learned from the Choctaws and Chickasaws. Then be sure to add the ingenuity, the creativity, and the keen taste of refugee Acadians who had to learn the use of nature's own food wherever these were to be found. Now, add the exotic taste and magic seasonings of the African cook. Voilà!"

All of this took centuries. And come to think of it, everything about the cooking of this region takes time. Cooking here is not something you hurry through just to fill your stomach. Question a Cajun or Creole cook about timing and the conversation goes something like this:

"How long do you cook your roux?"

"Until it's just right."

"How many hours should the fish stock simmer?"

"Maybe all day."

"When is your gumbo ready?"

"About supper time."

The message is simple: Don't hurry. Mimic the Cajuns, who took 100 years just getting to the South,

PRECEDING OVERLEAF: A lone fisherman tries his luck on the Gulf Coast at Atchafalaya Bay, Louisiana.

ABOVE: Crawfish, a freshwater cousin of shrimp and lobster, is an essential ingredient in many Cajun dishes.

superimposing methods and cooking styles along the way. They departed their native Atlantic coast of France sometime in the seventeenth-century and settled in Nova Scotia, (the word "Cajun" comes from "Acadian"). At that point, their cooking had a decidedly French country touch, embellished by the generous use of seafood.

Seafood, wild game, and other produce were abundant, and a century passed quite happily and quickly. But the Acadians refused allegiance to the British Crown, which ultimately forced their expulsion. Sent packing, they worked their way down river to Louisiana, finding ingredients they had left behind: seafood, game, and enough herbs and spices to make any Cajun dish sing. Old ways soon gave way to new recipes, as the Cajuns intertwined with local Indians, Africans, Spaniards and Italians in the area. Those two centuries produced Cajun cuisine, the provocative blend of flavors that is often called "country cooking."

Despite the similarities between Cajun and Creole cuisines, they are really quite different. At least they started out that way. A true Creole descends from the original French and Spanish settlers in the South. Yet, a few hundred years of mingling with other groups added new blood to this ancestry. Today Creole cooking blends French, Spanish, Anglo-Saxon, black, and Indian influences. Like the ethnic mix that it is, the savory dishes are subtle, flavorful blends of seasonings and flavors, none dominating, each complementing the other.

Witness a Cajun or Creole creating a crayfish etouffé, and you begin to grasp the essence of this highly individual cuisine. You also begin to realize the ethnic influences at play. An etouffé (which means

TOP: *Overhung with Spanish moss, the hazy bayous of Louisiana have long exerted a mysterious fascination on the whole country.*
ABOVE: *The flamingo typifies Louisiana's distinctive, colorful wildlife.*

"smothered," by the way) embraces at least two of the classic ingredients of Cajun cooking: fish stock and roux. The fish stock requires hours of simmering and spares nothing: the crayfish, shrimp heads, and shells join the onion, celery, carrots, and seasonings in the pot.

With the heady stock made, the chef tackles the true backbone of many a Cajun or Creole dish—roux. Roux in the European-American style generally means a thickening agent made by lightly cooking flour and butter together, providing the basis for all white sauces. In Cajun it is taken one dramatic step beyond: browned just to the point of burning. As the roux turns reddish-brown, it is whisked off the stove and other ingredients are quickly stirred in and cooked in the still-searing, molten mass. This nut-brown "Cajun napalm," as Prudhomme calls it, thickens and adds a remarkable deep, earthy flavor to the dish.

LEFT: A veteran bayou fisherman uses age-old methods to net his catch.
RIGHT: Peppers, in all their varieties, find their way into most Cajun dishes.

The addition of green bell peppers, onion, celery, and garlic to the etouffé is a decidedly southern French or even Provençal touch. The shrimp come courtesy of the nearby Gulf, and the crawfish are from fresh inland waters. For peppery seasonings, the Deep South chef chooses from red and green peppers and chilies, like Anaheims, Louisiana ports, serranos, torridos, jalapeños, Bahamian reds, and even green tabascos. Scarlet red cayenne is a must. With all this emphasis on hot, you begin to get the idea the Deep South likes to scorch throats. "Where else would they refer to red pepper as 'a burn' "? asks a New Orleans chef.

All this is not to suggest that everyone in the Deep South cooks Cajun, Creole or even hot. In the brick and wrought iron restaurants of the French Quarter, you're apt to encounter classic Southern dishes. She-crab soup with its salty touch of crab eggs, roast game birds with oyster and corn bread stuffing, turtle soup, oysters Rockefeller (invented at the turn of the century at the famous Antoine's Restaurant), and perhaps a dessert of crunchy pecan pie can all be found. Strong black coffee, accented by chicory, finishes off the meal.

Down-home cooking can challenge the palate as well: heaping platters of boiled crawfish, okra soup, black-eyed peas, and red-eye gravy. And what of soul food, rib-sticking vittles born of scarcity? This might be a dinner of fried catfish topped with that garlicky mayonnaise called remoulade, hush puppies fried to a crisp golden yellow, and heaps of steaming collard greens.

It is no wonder that one region could produce such a tempting variety of cooking styles. The natural ingredients seem endless. Locals often bemoan the loss of the old French Market in New Orleans, where vegetable men would cry, "Get your twelve greens, lady!"

referring to the number of greens used in an herb gumbo. Fishmongers, wearing their rubber boots and aprons, would wave wiggling crabs and crawfish. But even the "new" market has its bounty: mounds of freshly caught redfish, red snapper, catfish, trout, flounder, and pompano await the buyer. Bright green okra, canary yellow corn, great bunches of turnip greens, leafy spinach, plump eggplants, and juicy peaches and pears are piled high to seduce the eye and palate.

Perhaps rice is the symbolic common denominator that ties it all together, somehow making sense of the culinary background that can only be described as crazy, eclectic, and simply delicious. Rice pervades the recipes of the Deep South. It all began with a single small bag of Madagascar rice brought to Charleston by an English sea captain in 1680. Within a few years, acres of rice were planted, much of it consumed right at home. Even today, Louisiana is one of the top rice producers in the United States. There, rice also crosses

The bayous yield a staggering wealth of fish and seafood.

class lines; it appears in satisfying red beans and rice and in delicate, flaky tarts at a formal tea. It becomes the vehicle for the flavors of jambalaya to cling to and forms a fluffy bed for peppery red gumbo.

Leon Soniat, nationally recognized writer and television chef from New Orleans, fondly remembers his grandmother, a fabulous New Orleans cook, saying,

"Creole cooking started with the French love of, and skill in, manipulating anything edible into a tasty dish. Then, if you combined this with the Spanish gust of piquancy, the native African ability for developing a slow cooking method to perfection, and the gift of herbs and spices from the Indians, you had the beginning of Creole cooking."

The gracious way of life of the antebellum South lives on in Louisiana, where entertaining others is a favorite pastime.

GREEN TURTLE SOUP

Recommended Wine: Chenin Blanc

6 TO 8 SERVINGS

2   *pounds green turtle meat, cut into pieces*
1   *large onion, peeled*
4   *whole cloves*
1   *bay leaf*
2   *teaspoons dried basil, crumbled*
2   *teaspoons dried marjoram, crumbled*
1   *teaspoon dried savory, crumbled*
1   *teaspoon dried thyme, crumbled*
    Salt
    Freshly ground pepper
¼   *cup all-purpose flour*
    Lemon slices, for garnish

In 5-quart Dutch oven, bring 3 quarts water and turtle meat to a boil over high heat. Pierce onion with cloves and add to pot. Add bay leaf, basil, marjoram, savory and thyme. Cover, reduce heat to low and simmer until meat is tender, about 3 hours.

Remove from heat and strain broth. When turtle meat is cool, dice meat.

Return broth and meat to Dutch oven and bring to a simmer over medium heat. Season to taste with salt and pepper.

In small bowl, combine flour with 1 cup water and stir until smooth. Gradually whisk flour mixture into soup and cook until thickened.

Serve hot, garnished with lemon slices.

LOUISIANA FILE GUMBO

Recommended Wine: Rosé of Cabernet

8 SERVINGS

1   *broiler/fryer chicken (3 to 4 pounds), cut up*
2   *bay leaves*
1   *teaspoon salt*
½   *teaspoon freshly ground pepper*
½   *teaspoon dried oregano, crumbled*
½   *teaspoon dried basil, crumbled*
½   *teaspoon dried thyme, crumbled*
½   *teaspoon paprika*
¼   *teaspoon cayenne pepper*
¼   *pound andouille or ground pork sausage*
1   *to 4 tablespoons vegetable oil*
6   *tablespoons all-purpose flour*
6   *cloves garlic, minced*
2   *medium onions, chopped*
2   *ribs celery, chopped*
2   *green bell peppers, seeded and chopped*
½   *cup loosely packed parsley, chopped*
    Finely grated zest of 1 lemon
½   *pound cooked crab meat*
½   *pound raw shrimp, shelled and deveined*
½   *pint chopped raw oysters, drained*
    Hot cooked white rice
2   *tablespoons filé powder*

PRECEDING OVERLEAF: The bounty of the sea results in Louisiana Filé Gumbo, as mouth-watering as it is eye-catching.

Place chicken pieces in 5-quart Dutch oven and add 3 quarts water to cover. Bring to a boil over high heat. Reduce heat to low, cover and simmer until chicken is tender, 1½ to 2 hours.

Remove from heat, place chicken in large bowl and strain broth over it. Cover bowl and refrigerate at once.

When chicken is cool, remove skin and bones and dice enough meat to measure 2 cups. Skim fat from chilled broth and discard.

Return broth to Dutch oven. Add bay leaves, salt, pepper, oregano, basil, thyme, paprika and cayenne. Bring to a boil over high heat. Reduce heat to low and simmer, uncovered, until broth is reduced to 2 quarts, about 30 minutes. Set aside; reserve Dutch oven.

Meanwhile, in small skillet, cook sausage over medium high heat, stirring frequently, until browned, 8 to 10 minutes. Remove sausage with a slotted spoon and set aside.

Measure drippings, adding oil, if necessary, to measure 3½ tablespoons. Stir flour into drippings in pan and cook over medium low heat, stirring constantly, until roux is richly browned, 35 to 45 minutes. Do not burn roux; use low heat and stir all the while. Remove from heat and set aside.

Place Dutch oven and remaining oil over medium heat. Add garlic, onions, celery, green bell peppers and parsley and sauté until vegetables are tender, 8 to 10 minutes.

Stir in roux and lemon zest. Gradually whisk in reserved chicken stock. Increase heat to high and bring to a boil. Reduce heat to low. Add reserved chicken and sausage and simmer, partially covered, for 1 to 2 hours.

Add crab meat, shrimp and oysters. Simmer until shrimp turns pink, about 5 minutes.

Serve gumbo in bowls over hot rice, and sprinkle each serving with filé powder.

HUSH PUPPIES

MAKES 4 DOZEN HUSH PUPPIES

1	cup self-rising flour	1	egg, lightly beaten
1	cup white cornmeal	1½	cups crème fraîche
¼	cup white sesame seeds	1	cup finely chopped onion
¼	teaspoon baking soda		Vegetable oil for frying
½	teaspoon salt	8	ounces lard
	Dash of cayenne pepper		

In medium bowl, combine flour, corn-meal, sesame seeds, baking soda, salt and cayenne; set aside.

In small bowl, stir together egg, crème fraîche and onion. All at once, pour wet ingredients into cornmeal mixture. Stir gently, just until blended.

Pour enough oil into 2- or 3-quart saucepan to reach a depth of about 2 inches. Add lard. Heat to 375 degrees.

Drop batter by tablespoonfuls into hot oil. Fry 6 to 8 hush puppies at a time, turning once, until richly browned on all sides, about 2 minutes. Drain on paper towels and serve hot.

CORN-CHUTNEY MUFFINS

MAKES 1 DOZEN MUFFINS

2   peaches, pared, halved and pitted
1/2   lemon, chopped
3   tablespoons white wine vinegar
1/2   cup plus 2 tablespoons sugar
1   clove garlic, crushed through a press
2   teaspoons minced fresh ginger root
     Salt
     Dash of cayenne pepper
1/4   teaspoon whole yellow mustard seed
1/4   teaspoon whole coriander seed
1/4   teaspoon whole allspice berries
2/3   cup yellow cornmeal
1 1/3 cups all-purpose flour
1   tablespoon plus 1 teaspoon baking
         powder
1   cup milk
2   eggs, lightly beaten
1/4   cup lard, melted

Coarsely chop peaches.

In medium nonreactive saucepan, combine peaches with lemon, vinegar, 2 tablespoons sugar, garlic, ginger, 1/8 teaspoon salt and pepper.

Place mustard, coriander and all-spice in a triple thickness of cheese-cloth and tie securely with string. Moisten with water and add to fruit mixture.

Simmer, uncovered, stirring occasionally, over medium heat until thick and syrupy, 40 to 45 minutes. Remove cheesecloth bag and set peach chutney aside.

Preheat oven to 400 degrees. Lightly grease twelve 2 1/2-inch muffin cups.

In medium bowl, combine corn-meal, flour, remaining 1/2 cup sugar, baking powder and 1/2 teaspoon salt. In another bowl, blend milk, eggs and melted lard. Pour all at once into cornmeal mixture and fold gently just until combined.

Spoon 2 tablespoons of batter into each greased muffin cup. Spoon 1 tablespoon peach chutney on top. Cover chutney with remaining batter.

Bake until lightly browned, about 15 minutes.

JOHNNY CAKE

8 SERVINGS

3/4   cup yellow cornmeal
1   cup all-purpose flour
1   teaspoon baking powder
1   teaspoon baking soda
1/2   teaspoon salt
3   tablespoons honey
1   egg, lightly beaten
3   tablespoons unsalted butter, melted
1 1/4   cups buttermilk

Preheat oven to 400 degrees. Generously grease a 9-inch square baking pan.

In large bowl, combine cornmeal, flour, baking powder, baking soda and salt.

In small bowl, combine honey, egg, butter and buttermilk. Add to cornmeal mixture and stir just until blended.

Pour into prepared pan and bake until a toothpick inserted near center comes out clean, 25 to 30 minutes. Remove from oven and cool on wire rack. Serve warm.

CORN, OKRA AND TOMATOES

6 SERVINGS

2   ears fresh sweet corn, husks and silk removed
1   large sweet onion, chopped
1   green bell pepper, seeded and chopped
2   cups okra, trimmed and sliced
2   tablespoons bacon fat
2   tomatoes, seeded and chopped
1/2   teaspoon salt
1/8   teaspoon freshly ground pepper

Cut kernels from corn cobs; set aside.

In large skillet over medium heat, sauté onion, bell pepper and okra in bacon fat until onion is soft, about 5 minutes. Add tomatoes, reserved corn, salt and pepper and cook until vegetables are tender, about 10 minutes.

STIR-FRIED MIXED GREENS

6 TO 8 SERVINGS

2   tablespoons peanut oil
1/4   cup bacon fat
1   bunch collard greens, cleaned and chopped (about 12 cups, loosely packed)
1   bunch mustard greens, cleaned and

chopped (about 12 cups, loosely packed)
1/2   teaspoon salt
1/4   teaspoon freshly ground pepper
2   tablespoons distilled white vinegar

Heat 1 tablespoon peanut oil and 2 tablespoons bacon fat in wok or 12-inch skillet over high heat. Add half of the collard greens, half the mustard greens, ¼ teaspoon salt and ⅛ teaspoon pepper. Stir-fry until vegetables are bright green and just wilted, about 1 minute.

Add 1 tablespoon of the vinegar; toss lightly. Transfer cooked greens to heated serving platter; keep warm.

Repeat with remaining ingredients. Serve hot.

DELTA RICE

Recommended Wine: Zinfandel

8 SERVINGS

¼   *pound sliced bacon, diced*
½   *pound chicken gizzards*
½   *pound chicken livers*
1   *medium onion, chopped*
1   *rib celery, chopped*
1   *small red bell pepper, seeded and diced*
1   *small yellow bell pepper, seeded and diced*
2   *tablespoons vegetable oil (optional)*
1   *tablespoon Creole or Dijon-style coarsely-ground prepared mustard*
1   *teaspoon salt*
1   *teaspoon dried thyme, crumbled*
1   *teaspoon dried oregano, crumbled*
½   *teaspoon freshly ground white pepper*
½   *teaspoon paprika*
¼   *teaspoon celery seed*
2½ *cups rich homemade chicken stock*
1   *cup long-grain rice*
½   *pint (8-ounces) extra-small shucked oysters, drained*

In large skillet, cook bacon over medium heat, stirring frequently, until crisp, 5 to 7 minutes. Remove from skillet and set aside.

Discard all but 2 tablespoons bacon drippings from skillet. Add gizzards to drippings and cook, turning once, until lightly browned, 3 to 5 minutes. Remove from skillet with slotted spoon and set aside.

Add livers to skillet and cook, turning once, until lightly browned, 3 to 5 minutes. Remove from skillet with slotted spoon and set aside.

Add onion, celery and bell peppers to skillet, along with vegetable oil if necessary. Sauté until onion is soft, about 3 minutes. Stir in mustard, salt, thyme, oregano, pepper, paprika and celery seed.

Finely mince gizzards and livers and return to skillet. Pour in chicken stock and bring to a boil over high heat. Stir in rice, cover and reduce heat to low. Cook until rice has absorbed all liquid, 20 to 25 minutes.

During last 5 minutes of cooking, place oysters on top of rice. Cover and cook until oysters are slightly firm and edges are curled, about 5 minutes.

Crumble reserved bacon and sprinkle on each serving.

Delta Rice and Red Beans are accompaniments to a host of classic Cajun dishes.

RED BEANS

8 TO 10 SERVINGS

1   pound dried red beans
1   pound meaty smoked ham hocks
1   green bell pepper, seeded and chopped
1   yellow bell pepper, seeded and chopped
1   red bell pepper, seeded and chopped
2   medium onions, chopped
4   cloves garlic, minced
½   cup chopped fresh parsley
2   bay leaves
1   teaspoon dried marjoram, crumbled
½   teaspoon dried thyme, crumbled

Rinse beans under cold running water.

Place in Dutch oven with all of remaining ingredients. Bring to a boil over high heat. Cover, reduce heat to low and simmer until beans are almost tender, about 45 minutes.

Remove ham hocks and set aside to cool. Cut pork from bones and chop. Return meat to pan and discard bones.

Continue cooking beans until tender, 30 to 45 minutes more. Remove bay leaves and serve hot.

SHIRRED EGGS WITH JARLSBERG GRITS

8 SERVINGS

1   quart milk
5   tablespoons unsalted butter
1   cup quick-cooking hominy grits
½   teaspoon salt
¼   teaspoon freshly ground white pepper
1   small clove garlic, minced
    Dash of freshly grated nutmeg
6   ounces Jarlsberg cheese, shredded
8   eggs
½   cup half-and-half
2   tablespoons chopped fresh tarragon
2   tablespoons freshly grated Parmesan
        cheese
8   tomato slices
    Freshly ground black pepper

Preheat oven to 350 degrees.

In 3-quart saucepan, bring milk and

4 tablespoons butter just to a boil over medium high heat. Slowly stir in grits. Reduce heat and simmer until grits are thick, about 5 minutes.

Stir in salt, white pepper, garlic, nutmeg and Jarlsberg cheese.

Pour grits into 8 lightly greased 10- or 12-ounce baking dishes.

Break and slip 1 egg into each baking dish. Spoon 1 tablespoon half-and-half over each serving. Dot eggs with remaining 1 tablespoon butter.

Bake until egg whites are set and yolks are soft and creamy, 15 to 20 minutes.

Meanwhile, in small bowl, combine tarragon and Parmesan. Place tomato slices side by side on baking sheet and top each slice with about 1½ teaspoons of tarragon mixture.

When eggs are cooked, change temperature to broil. Broil tomatoes 4 to 5 inches from heat until lightly browned, about 2 minutes.

Before serving, top each baking dish with a broiled tomato slice and season with black pepper.

In Louisiana, even Shirred Eggs with Jarlsberg Grits are well-seasoned—with garlic and fresh tarragon.

DUCK AND EGGPLANT JAMBALAYA

Recommended Wine: Merlot

8 SERVINGS

1   medium duck (3½ to 4 pounds)
2   whole onions, trimmed plus 2 medium
        onions, chopped
6   whole cloves
2   carrots, trimmed
2   ribs celery, trimmed
6   whole allspice berries
6   whole black peppercorns
1   pound andouille sausage, sliced
3   cloves garlic, minced
3   shallots, minced
2   green bell peppers, seeded and chopped
1   bay leaf
1   teaspoon dried thyme, crumbled
1   teaspoon ground cumin
½   teaspoon cayenne pepper
¼   teaspoon ground cloves
1½   cups long-grain white rice
½   cup wild rice
1   eggplant, peeled and cut into 1-inch
        cubes
⅓   cup all-purpose flour
     Lime wedges, for garnish

Preheat oven to 350 degrees.

Remove skin from duck and place in large baking dish. Bake until fat is rendered, about 30 minutes.

Pour drippings into heatproof bowl; discard skin.

Meanwhile, cut duck into 8 serving pieces. Remove breast from bone and reserve meat. Place bones and duck trimmings in 6-quart stockpot and cover with about 5 quarts water. Stud whole onions with cloves and add to pot. Add carrots, celery, allspice and peppercorns.

Cover and bring to a boil over high heat. Reduce heat and simmer for 2 to 3 hours.

Remove from heat and strain broth into large bowl. Discard solids. Cover broth and refrigerate at once.

Skim fat from chilled broth and discard. Return broth to clean stockpot and bring to a boil over high heat. Boil until reduced to 1 quart.

Meanwhile, in 5-quart Dutch oven, sauté andouille in 2 tablespoons reserved duck fat, turning frequently, until browned, 5 to 7 minutes. Transfer to paper towels to drain; set aside.

Add garlic, shallots, chopped onions, bell peppers, bay leaf, thyme, cumin, cayenne and ground cloves to Dutch oven, adding more duck fat, if necessary. Sauté, stirring frequently, until lightly browned; about 10 minutes.

Stir in reduced duck broth, white rice and wild rice. Cover, reduce heat to low and cook for 15 minutes.

Meanwhile, heat 2 tablespoons duck fat in large skillet over high heat. Add eggplant and sauté until lightly browned on all sides, about 5 minutes. Transfer to plate and set aside.

Andouille sausage helps to give Duck and Eggplant Jambalaya its distinctive flavor.

Dredge reserved duck breast in flour, shaking off excess. Add breast and duck pieces to skillet and cook, turning frequently, until browned and tender, about 10 minutes.

After rice has cooked for 15 min-utes, add eggplant, duck and an-douille to Dutch oven. Gently stir mixture, cover and continue cooking until rice is tender, about 10 minutes more.

To serve, garnish with lime wedges.

RABBIT DIJON WITH LEEKS AND WILD MUSHROOMS

Recommended Wine: Cabernet Sauvignon

6 SERVINGS

½	pound pancetta (smoked Italian bacon)
1	cup all-purpose flour
½	teaspoon salt
¼	teaspoon freshly ground pepper
1	large rabbit (4½ to 5 pounds) skinned and cut into 6 serving pieces
1	quart rich homemade chicken stock, warmed
¼	teaspoon sage leaves
1	cup heavy cream
2	tablespoons Dijon-style mustard
6	leeks, well washed and white part sliced
1	pound fresh wild mushrooms, sliced

Preheat oven to 375 degrees.

Cut pancetta into 1-inch dice. Place in 2-quart baking dish and bake until fat is rendered and pancetta is crisp, about 30 minutes.

Remove from oven and reduce heat to 225 degrees. Transfer pancetta to paper towels to drain; set aside. Set drippings aside.

In medium bowl, combine flour, salt and pepper. Dredge rabbit pieces in flour mixture, shaking off excess. Reserve flour mixture for gravy. In large deep skillet, heat 3 tablespoons of pancetta drippings over medium high heat. Add rabbit pieces and cook, turning frequently, until browned and fork-tender, 20 to 30 minutes.

Transfer to serving platter and re-serve skillet. Keep rabbit warm in oven while preparing Dijon sauce.

Stir 3 tablespoons of reserved flour mixture into drippings that remain in skillet. Cook over medium heat, scraping up browned bits from bottom of pan, about 3 minutes. Slowly whisk in chicken stock and sage. Simmer, stirring frequently, until mixture thick-ens and is reduced by half.

Stir in cream and mustard.

In large skillet over medium high heat, sauté leeks in 1 tablespoon reserved pancetta drippings until soft and lightly browned, 3 to 4 minutes. Stir into reduced Dijon sauce.

Add 1 tablespoon reserved pancetta drippings to skillet and add mush-rooms. Sauté until just warmed through, about 1 minute.

To serve, arrange rabbit pieces on platter. Spoon Dijon sauce over rabbit and garnish with wild mushrooms.

BAYOU CHICKEN

Recommended Wine: Pinot Noir

6 SERVINGS

3   whole skinless, boneless chicken breasts,
       split
²⁄₃ cup white rum
2   tablespoons unsalted butter
    Freshly ground pepper
2   tablespoons peanut oil
1   large shallot, minced
1   cup chopped roasted unsalted peanuts,

       skins removed
¹⁄₂ teaspoon salt
¹⁄₄ teaspoon paprika
¹⁄₈ to ¹⁄₄ teaspoon cayenne pepper
2   cups rich homemade chicken stock
    Juice of 1 lime
    Hot cooked white rice

Bayou Chicken evokes the smells and flavors of the Deep South.

Place chicken breast fillets between 2 sheets of plastic wrap and pound with meat mallet until ¼ inch thick. Place chicken fillets in glass dish or re-closable plastic bag. Pour rum over chicken and turn to coat. Cover dish or close bag and refrigerate, turning occasionally, 8 hours or overnight.

Preheat oven to 225 degrees.

Drain chicken, reserving marinade for sauce.

In large skillet, melt butter over medium-high heat. Add chicken fillets and sauté, turning once, until lightly browned, 3 to 5 minutes. Season to taste with pepper.

Transfer chicken to platter and keep warm in oven while preparing sauce.

Add peanut oil to drippings in skillet. Add shallot and sauté until tender, about 3 minutes. Stir in pea-nuts, salt, paprika and cayenne. Cook, stirring constantly, until peanuts turn golden, about 5 minutes.

Stir in broth and bring to a boil over high heat. Reduce heat to low and simmer until peanuts become soft, about 10 minutes. Remove from heat.

Strain mixture through cheesecloth-lined sieve and return sauce to skillet. Purée sieved peanut mixture in food mill and return purée to skillet. Gently heat over low heat; stir in lime juice.

To serve, spoon sauce over chicken and rice.

DRY MARINATED SPARE RIBS

Recommended Wine: Zinfandel

6 TO 8 SERVINGS

2   tablespoons whole black peppercorns
1   tablespoon celery seed
1   tablespoon salt
1   tablespoon garlic powder
2   teaspoons onion powder
2   teaspoons paprika
1   teaspoon dried mint leaves, crumbled
4   bay leaves
9   pounds pork spareribs

In blender or food processor, combine peppercorns, celery seed, salt, garlic powder, onion powder, paprika, mint and bay leaves. Process to a fine powder.

Sprinkle both sides of ribs with spice powder.

Wrap ribs in a double thickness of heavy-duty aluminum foil and seal well. Refrigerate for 12 to 24 hours.

Prepare charcoal, gas or electric grill. Arrange ribs 4 to 6 inches above medium-low heat. Grill slowly, turning occasionally, until ribs are browned and tender, 2½ to 3½ hours total cooking time.

Cut into serving pieces. Serve hot.

BREAD PUDDING WITH APRICOT-FIG WHISKEY COMPOTE

Recommended Wine: Muscat Canelli

8 SERVINGS

1½ cups fresh or canned coconut milk
2½ cups half-and-half
4   eggs
½   cup sugar
½   cup honey
2   tablespoons vanilla extract
⅛   teaspoon ground cinnamon
⅛   teaspoon freshly grated nutmeg
8   cups cubed dry brioche (from about 8 rolls)
1   pound dried figs
2   pounds fresh apricots
½   cup whiskey
2   tablespoons dark corn syrup
1   cinnamon stick
½   vanilla bean, split

In large bowl, combine coconut milk, half-and-half, eggs, sugar, honey, vanilla extract, cinnamon and nutmeg. Gently fold in cubed brioche. Cover and refrigerate for 8 hours or overnight.

Preheat oven to 350 degrees.

Turn mixture into lightly greased 13 × 9 × 2-inch baking dish. Bake until knife inserted near center comes out clean, 55 to 60 minutes.

While pudding is baking, prepare Apricot-Fig Whiskey Compote: Slice figs and pit and slice apricots. In heavy 2-quart saucepan, combine figs, apricots, whiskey, corn syrup, cinnamon stick and vanilla bean. Bring to a boil over high heat. Cover, reduce heat to low and simmer until figs are tender, about 30 minutes. Remove and discard cinnamon stick and vanilla bean.

To serve, spoon warm compote over bread pudding.

OVERLEAF: After a spicy gumbo or crawfish etouffé, there's nothing like a piece of sweet Pecan Pie with Nutty Pastry to please the palate.

PECAN PIE WITH NUTTY PASTRY

8 SERVINGS

6   tablespoons unsalted butter, at room
      temperature
1   cup firmly packed dark brown sugar
4   eggs, lightly beaten
1¼ cups dark corn syrup
1   teaspoon vanilla extract
⅛   teaspoon salt
1   cup coarsely chopped pecans plus ½ cup
      pecan halves
      Nutty Pastry (recipe follows)

Preheat oven to 350 degrees.

In medium bowl, cream butter and sugar with an electric mixer at high speed.

Beat in eggs, one at a time, beating well after each addition

Beat in corn syrup, vanilla and salt; mix well. Stir in chopped pecans.

On lightly floured surface, roll out pastry dough ⅛ inch thick. Fit pastry gently into 9-inch pie plate. Trim and flute edge.

Pour filling into pie shell; arrange pecan halves on top. Bake in pre-heated oven until pastry is light brown and filling is firm in the center, 45 to 50 minutes.

Remove from oven and cool on wire rack. Cover; chill before serving. Serve garnished with whipped cream and finely chopped pecans, if desired.

NUTTY PASTRY

MAKES ONE 9-INCH SINGLE CRUST PIE SHELL

1   cup plus 2 tablespoons all-purpose flour
¼   teaspoon salt
¼   cup finely chopped pecans
2   tablespoons unsalted butter, chilled and
      cut into pieces.
¼   cup solid vegetable shortening, chilled
      and cut into pieces
2   to 3 tablespoons ice water

In medium bowl, stir together flour, salt and pecans. Cut in butter and

shortening with pastry blender or 2 knives until mixture resembles coarse crumbs.

Sprinkle on 2 tablespoons water and mix lightly with fork until dough begins to stick together. Add more water if needed. Press dough into ball.

Wrap in plastic wrap and refrigerate until ready to use.

CASHAW PIE

6 SERVINGS

Orange Pastry (recipe follows)
2 cups mashed, cooked cashaw squash or pumpkin
¾ cup scalded milk, cooled
3 eggs
¼ cup sugar
2 tablespoons molasses
1 teaspoon ground cinnamon
1 to 2 teaspoons grated orange zest
½ teaspoon freshly grated nutmeg
¼ teaspoon ground ginger
⅛ teaspoon ground cloves
Whipped cream, optional

Prepare Orange Pastry and set aside.

Preheat oven to 450 degrees.

In large mixing bowl, combine cashaw, milk, eggs, sugar, molasses, cinnamon, orange zest, nutmeg, ginger and cloves. Beat with electric mixer at medium speed for 3 minutes; set aside.

Roll dough out on lightly floured surface to ⅛-inch thick. Fit pastry gently into 9-inch pie plate. Trim and flute edge.

Pour cashaw mixture into pie shell.

Bake for 10 minutes. Reduce heat to 350 degrees and bake until a knife inserted near center comes out clean, 45 to 50 minutes.

Serve warm or chilled, cut into wedges and garnished with whipped cream, if desired.

ORANGE PASTRY

MAKES ONE 9-INCH SINGLE CRUST PIE SHELL

1⅓ cups all-purpose flour
¼ teaspoon salt
½ cup solid vegetable shortening, chilled and cut into pieces
¼ cup frozen orange juice concentrate, thawed

In medium bowl combine flour and salt. Cut in shortening with pastry blender or 2 knives until mixture resembles coarse crumbs.

Sprinkle orange juice concentrate over flour mixture. Mix lightly with fork until dough begins to stick together. Press dough into ball.

Wrap in plastic wrap and refrigerate until ready to use.

THE
MID-ATLANTIC

RECIPES

From north to south, Chesapeake Bay stretches 200 miles, from the Susquehanna River delta near the Pennsylvania-Maryland border to the point northeast of Norfolk, Virginia, where it empties into the Atlantic. All along the Bay's length, labyrinthine marshes and tributaries branch and flare to the east and west, creating this continent's largest estuary, which has inspired and supported culinary exploration from the earliest times.

The first colonists sailed into the Bay in 1607, heading 40 miles up the James River to a point they christened Jamestown. Captain John Smith wrote, "Heaven and earth never agreed better to frame a place for man's habitation," and in fact the land overflowed with corn, beans, onions, and other crops cultivated by the Indians, as well as delicious wild fruits, nuts, and berries. The woods teemed with life—deer, squirrel, rabbit, opossum, and bear—and the marshes were home to turkeys, quail, ducks, geese, widgeons, and pigeons. But in the first difficult years, when they were often too weak to hunt or tend crops, it was the bounty of the Bay itself that kept the newcomers from starving.

The Bay has offered up its abundance in prodigious quantities ever since. Fed by 5 major rivers, encompassing more than 4,500 miles of shoreline, and home to more than 2,700 different species of mammals, birds, fish, and reptiles, it supplies, to cite but one example, fully half the nation's harvest of Atlantic blue crabs. These are plucked, netted, potted, scraped, and dredged from its waters in numbers averaging between 150 and 240 million annually. The total annual catch—including harvests of oysters, clams, striped bass, her-ring, shad, perch, drum, trout, puffer, and eel, to name only a few—reaches an astonishing 400 million pounds. Scant surprise then that regional cooking, now as always, reflects this estuarial treasure-trove with endless variations on crab cakes and clam fritters, fish chowders, and terrapin stews.

Still, for sheer versatility and popularity, one Bay resident stands (or sits) supreme: the oyster. It was undoubtedly its oysters that Oliver Wendell Holmes was saluting when he dubbed Baltimore "the gastronomic capital of the universe." Our national passion for the spunky bivalve, rekindled in recent years, verged on madness in the nineteenth century. As early as the 1820s, entire oyster caravans rolled west out of Baltimore, their precious cargo packed in seawater-soaked hay. By stagecoach, canal boat, wagon, and train, fresh oysters traveled inland to Cincinnati, Chicago, and eventually St. Louis, where eager crowds awaited the opportunity to pay small fortunes for them.

In coastal cities, however, the magnificent mollusks were anything but a rarity. Oyster vendors shucked and

PRECEDING OVERLEAF: The Mid-Atlantic states are a land of bountiful farms and rolling hills. Before the arrival of European colonists, the region supported a vast array of wildlife.

ABOVE: A tranquil scene in rural West Virginia.

jived on every corner, and oyster saloons—where a hungry laborer could down unlimited quantities for as little as 6 cents—were the fast-food outlets of the day. Men, women, and whole families gulped them with beer and dipped them in ketchup and consumed them in stuffings, pies, scallops, and stews. They were gobbled up in such quantities that the Chesapeake Bay, which had been steadily producing up to 17 million bushels of oysters a year, was tapped out by the turn of the century. Today, after years of patient cultivation and a heartening turnaround in pollution-control measures, oysters are again a principal year-round product, but in numbers less than one-fifth of those of the past.

Modern-day oyster roasts, the area's versions of the New England clambake, remain a popular reminder of the antebellum feasts that gave rise to the term "Southern hospitality." In those vanished days, barrels of oysters, spread out to roast, served only as an introduction to enormous meals that lasted for hours and included as many as six or seven different meats, game birds, and fish.

It is almost impossible for us today to comprehend the magnitude of the feasting that marked the daily lives of the plantation aristocracy from the late seventeenth century on. By that time the plantation owners of Tidewater Virginia had already amassed great fortunes, built on the economics of slave labor and the new-found European addiction to tobacco. Their lives were given over to luxury and power: a privileged potpourri of politics, horse racing, beautiful furnishings, fine food, and imported wines. Governor William Berkeley's famous description of Virginia as "the land of good eating, good drinking, stout men, and pretty women" is as pithy and accurate as any.

TOP: *Fishing boats docked in the quiet harbor of Tilghman Island, Maryland. The state's waters teem with countless varieties of fish and shellfish.*

ABOVE: *Maryland crabs are a regional delicacy.*

Large estates, modeled after English country manors, were in fact small villages. Typically, they would comprise several dozen buildings, from carpenter's and blacksmith's shops to icehouses, smokehouses, and dairies. Lavish cooking built upon elaborate experimentation in orchard, vineyard and, garden was the rule. And no one pursued his epicurean interests more fervently than Thomas Jefferson, who transplanted cuttings from European vineyards and orchards, cultivated an enormous variety of vegetables in his meticulous gardens, and is even credited with the first written recipe for ice cream. Jefferson's fondness for European (particularly French) food and wine was almost equaled by his love of native American cooking, and he delighted in marrying the two. The lucky guest invited to dine at his table could expect an eclectic feast of Bay seafood and fresh garden vegetables, *boeuf à la daube* and Virginia ham, wild turkey, and fine French wines.

For Jefferson and the generations who preceded and followed him, pork was the cornerstone on which all meals were built. Hogs ran wild, required no care, grew

TOP LEFT: A Chesapeake Bay waterman plies his trade.

TOP RIGHT: A Virginia farmer harvests his crop.

ABOVE: Fresh poultry adds diversity to Mid-Atlantic cooking.

rapidly, and were infinitely adaptable. In the planters' smokehouses and kitchens they were used to make everything from roasts, sausages, and bacon to chitterlings, or chitlins, the original soul food. It was Virginia ham, specifically the famous Smithfield ham, that stood as the *pièce de résistance.*

The original Smithfields borrowed their recipe from the Chinese, using lean, half-wild razorback hogs fed on acorns, hickory nuts, and, for at least their final weeks, peanuts. The time-honored Smithfield process of dry salt curing, hickory smoking, and slow aging, still in use today, takes anywhere from nine to twenty-one months. The finished ham will last virtually forever. Other hams, from towns and counties scattered throughout Kentucky, Tennessee, and the Carolinas, gain their distinctive flavors from innumerable local variations on the process. The merits of the hams themselves, as well as the recipes for boiling and roasting them, are still vigorously and frequently debated.

A fine Southern ham is customarily accompanied by relishes or sweet dishes such as pickled watermelon

LEFT: *September is apple-harvesting time in the Mid-Atlantic states.*
RIGHT: *On a bluff overlooking the Potomac River, Mount Vernon, George Washington's elegant home, symbolizes the gracious way of life of the early landowners in the Mid-Atlantic states.*

rinds. And certainly no traditional table is complete without a pot of fresh greens—turnip, mustard, collard, or dandelion, slow cooked with fatback or a ham hock into a dish known simply as "mess o' greens and potlikker"—a Southern trademark dating back to the days of slavery.

Invented out of necessity by black cooks with a talent for extracting the most flavor from the humblest ingredients, soul food, which also boasted staples such as black-eyed peas, grits, fried yams, and sweet potato puddings and pies, was to become the most imag-inative—and popular—style of regional cooking from the Bay all the way down to the Gulf.

For more than two centuries, soul food was the living embodiment of down-home Southern cooking. It anticipated the current fashion for varied spicy salad greens, home-grown produce and grilled, wood-smoked meats. And, in the broader sense, it defined a natural, unpretentious approach to good eating that brought fresh foods and good company to the dinner table.

The vegetable garden at Mount Vernon.

MARINATED BAY SCALLOPS WITH GREEN BEANS

Recommended Wine: Sauvignon Blanc

10 SERVINGS

1	pound bay scallops
2	teaspoons grated lime zest
	Juice of 6 limes
2	teaspoons prepared horseradish
1	pound fresh green beans, French-cut
	Juice of 1/2 lemon
2	tablespoons olive oil
1/2	teaspoon salt
1/4	teaspoon freshly ground pepper

Rinse scallops and pat dry with paper towels. In medium nonreactive bowl, combine lime zest, lime juice and horseradish. Add scallops and stir to coat. Cover and refrigerate for 6 hours, or overnight, stirring occasionally.

In large saucepan over medium heat, bring 1-inch of salted water to a boil. Add beans, reduce heat to low, cover and simmer until crisp-tender, about 3 minutes. Drain and transfer to medium bowl.

Sprinkle with lemon juice, olive oil, salt and pepper. Toss lightly. Cover and refrigerate for 6 hours, or overnight, stirring occasionally.

To serve, arrange chilled beans on large serving platter. Drain scallops and discard marinade. Thread 4 to 6 scallops on each of ten 6-inch wooden or bamboo skewers and arrange on top of green beans.

Serve chilled.

CRAB CAKES

Recommended Wine: Chardonnay

MAKES 2 DOZEN CRAB CAKES

2	cloves garlic, minced		1/4	teaspoon freshly ground white pepper
2	tablespoons minced shallots			Dash of cayenne pepper
2	tablespoons unsalted butter		2	eggs, lightly beaten
1	pound (about 3 cups) cooked crab meat		2	cups fine dry bread crumbs
1/4	cup mayonnaise			About 2 cups peanut oil
2	tablespoons heavy cream			About 2 cups corn oil
1/4	cup chopped fresh parsley			Lemon wedges, for serving
1/4	teaspoon dried thyme, crumbled			

The scallops of Chesapeake Bay are fabled for their delicate flavor and buttery texture.
Marinating in lime juice for several hours is an easy way to "cook" them.

Marinated Bay Scallops with Green Beans.

In small skillet over medium heat, sauté garlic and shallots in butter for 30 seconds.

In large bowl, combine sautéed vegetables, crab meat, mayonnaise, cream, parsley, thyme, pepper and cayenne. Divide mixture into 2 dozen 2-tablespoon portions. Shape into cylinders, about 1½ inches in diameter.

In small shallow bowl, beat eggs with 1 tablespoon water. Pour bread crumbs into pie plate.

One at a time, dip crab cakes in egg mixture then coat evenly with crumbs, placing crab cakes in a single layer on a baking sheet.

Cover lightly with waxed paper; refrigerate for 1 to 2 hours.

In 10-inch electric skillet or 4-quart saucepan, combine equal parts of peanut and corn oils to a depth of 1 inch. Heat to 375 degrees on deep-fat thermometer.

Add crab cakes, a few at a time, and cook, turning once, until richly browned, 35 to 45 seconds on each side. Drain thoroughly on paper towels.

Serve crab cakes at once, with lemon wedges.

ROAST CHESTNUT SOUP

Recommended Wine: Semillon

6 TO 8 SERVINGS

1	*pound fresh chestnuts*
½	*cup chopped onion*
1	*cup chopped celery*
3	*tablespoons unsalted butter*
1½	*quarts rich homemade chicken broth*
1	*bay leaf*
1	*cup half-and-half*
½	*teaspoon salt*
¼	*teaspoon freshly ground white pepper*
	Dash of freshly grated nutmeg

Preheat oven to 400 degrees.

Using a sharp knife, slash chestnut shells. Place chestnuts on a baking sheet and roast for 15 minutes.

When cool, remove shells and inner skins.

In 3-quart saucepan over medium-high heat, sauté onion and celery in butter until soft.

Add chestnuts, chicken broth and bay leaf and bring to boil over high heat. Reduce heat to low and cook until chestnuts are tender, about 15 minutes. Remove bay leaf.

In blender or food processor fitted with a metal blade, purée soup until smooth.

Return soup to pan; stir in half-and-half, salt, pepper and nutmeg. Heat through over low heat. Serve hot.

SOFT PRETZELS

MAKES 16 PRETZELS

1¼ cups lukewarm water (110°F. to
    115°F.)
2½ teaspoons sugar
1   package (1 tablespoon) active dry yeast
2   tablespoons unsalted butter, melted
1   teaspoon salt
3   to 4 cups all-purpose flour
3   tablespoons baking soda
1   egg yolk
¼   cup coarse salt
    A selection of prepared mustards, for
    serving

In large bowl, combine ¼ cup lukewarm water, ½ teaspoon sugar and yeast. Stir to dissolve yeast. Set aside until bubbly, about 5 minutes.

Stir in remaining 1 cup lukewarm water, 2 teaspoons sugar, butter, salt and 3 cups all-purpose flour.

Turn dough onto a lightly floured surface and knead until smooth and elastic, 8 to 10 minutes, adding more flour, if needed, to prevent dough from sticking.

Shape dough into a ball. Place in lightly oiled bowl, turning to coat all sides. Cover and let rise in warm place until doubled in bulk, about 1 hour.

Punch down dough and knead briefly. Divide into 16 equal pieces and shape into balls. Cover and let rest for about 10 minutes.

In a large saucepan, bring 2 quarts water to a bare simmer over medium-low heat. Stir in baking soda; keep warm.

Lightly grease 2 baking sheets. Roll each ball between your palms to form a long rope about 18 inches long. Dip rope into the warm baking soda solution then form into a pretzel shape on a baking sheet. Pinch ends to seal well. Repeat with remaining dough.

Cover and let pretzels rise until not quite doubled, about 25 minutes.

Preheat oven to 400 degrees.

In a small bowl, combine egg yolk with 1 tablespoon water. Brush pretzels with egg wash and sprinkle with coarse salt.

Bake until golden brown, about 15 minutes. Immediately transfer pretzels to a wire rack.

Serve warm with mustard.

For an authentic Pennsylvania Dutch treat, serve Soft Pretzels warm with a variety of mustards.

RYE BREAD

MAKES 2 LOAVES

1   *package (1 tablespoon) active dry yeast*
¾   *cup lukewarm water (110°F. to 115°F.)*
2   *cups rye flour*
1   *cup whole wheat flour*
3   *cups all-purpose flour*
1   *cup beer, at room temperature*
1   *egg*
¼   *cup walnut oil*
2   *teaspoons salt*

In large bowl, dissolve yeast in lukewarm water. Set aside until bubbly, about 5 minutes.

In large bowl, combine rye flour, whole wheat flour and 2 cups all-purpose flour; set aside.

Stir beer into yeast mixture. Using an electric mixer at medium speed, beat in 2½ cups of the flour mixture until smooth, about 2 minutes. (If not using a mixer, beat 300 strokes by hand.)

Cover and let rise until doubled in bulk, about 30 minutes.

Beat in egg, oil and salt. Stir in remaining flour mixture to make a stiff dough.

Turn dough onto lightly floured board. Knead until smooth and elastic, 8 to 10 minutes, adding all-purpose flour, if needed, to prevent dough from sticking.

Shape dough into a ball and place in lightly oiled bowl, turning to oil all sides. Cover and let rise in a warm place until doubled in bulk, about 1½ hours.

Punch down dough. Cover and let rise in warm place until doubled in bulk, about 1½ hours.

Punch down again, cover and let rest 10 minutes.

Turn dough out onto lightly floured surface and divide in half. Shape each half into a 10 × 4-inch oval loaf.

Place loaves on a lightly greased baking sheet. Cut 2 diagonal slashes, each 3 inches long, on the top of each loaf using very sharp knife or razor blade.

Cover and let rise until doubled in bulk, about 45 minutes.

Preheat oven to 400 degrees.

Place shallow pan of boiling water on bottom shelf of hot oven. Brush loaves lightly with water and bake on middle shelf, brushing with water twice more during baking, until loaves are browned and sound hollow when lightly tapped with fingers, about 45 minutes. Remove from baking sheet and cool on wire rack.

SCRAPPLE

8 SERVINGS

6   cups rich homemade chicken broth
1   medium onion, chopped
½   pound ground pork, crumbled
1   teaspoon salt
1   teaspoon dried sage leaves
¾   teaspoon dried marjoram
½   teaspoon dried thyme
¼   teaspoon freshly ground white pepper
⅛   teaspoon ground cloves
1¼   cups yellow cornmeal
2   tablespoons vegetable oil

In 5-quart Dutch oven, bring chicken broth to a boil over medium high heat.

Add onion and pork, and stir to break up pork. Add salt, sage, marjoram, thyme, pepper and cloves.

Reduce heat and simmer until pork is no longer pink, about 5 minutes.

Return broth to a boil and gradually add cornmeal over high heat, stirring constantly, until thick. Continue to cook and stir until mixture is thick and smooth, about 5 minutes.

Pour scrapple into 9 × 5 × 3-inch loaf pan. Cover and refrigerate until set, about 2 hours.

Cut scrapple into ½-inch slices.

Heat oil in large skillet over medium-high heat. Pan-fry scrapple slices until heated through, turning once, 1 to 2 minutes on each side. Serve hot.

Newport Coleslaw—a tangy and easy-to-prepare side dish.

NEWPORT COLESLAW

Recommended Wine: Rosé of Cabernet

6 SERVINGS

*Pickled Green Peppercorn Mayonnaise
    (recipe follows)*
2   *cups shredded carrots*
1   *large head Savoy cabbage, shredded
    (about 8 cups)*
½   *cup chopped sweet onion*
1   *to 2 tablespoons white wine vinegar
    Salt
    Freshly ground pepper*

1   *tablespoon caraway seeds, for garnish*

In large bowl, combine Pickled Green Peppercorn Mayonnaise, carrot, cabbage, onion and vinegar. Toss lightly. Season to taste with salt and pepper.

Cover and refrigerate to blend flavors, about 1 hour. Serve chilled. Garnish with caraway seeds, if desired.

PICKLED GREEN PEPPERCORN MAYONNAISE

MAKES 1¼ CUPS

1¼ *cups safflower oil*
1   *egg*
1   *tablespoon white wine vinegar*
2   *teaspoons green peppercorns packed in
    brine*
2   *teaspoons Dijon-style mustard*
½   *teaspoon salt*

In blender or food processor, combine ¼ cup oil with the egg, vinegar, peppercorns, mustard and salt until blended, about 5 seconds.

With machine running, gradually add remaining oil in a steady stream. Continue blending until well mixed and thickened.

STEAMED BEET GREENS

6 SERVINGS

3   *bunches beet greens*
2   *tablespoons white wine vinegar*
1   *clove garlic, crushed through a press*

Wash and trim beet greens.

Steam greens, covered, over boiling water in 3-quart saucepan until tender, about 3 minutes.

Drain; arrange on warmed serving platter. Drizzle with vinegar and garlic and toss lightly. Serve hot.

BEEFSTEAK TOMATO-EGGPLANT SALAD

6 SERVINGS

1   large eggplant (about 2 pounds)
½   pound pearl onions
1½   pounds large beefsteak tomatoes
       (about 3)
4   cups loosely packed chopped fresh basil
⅓   cup olive oil
⅓   cup red wine vinegar
2   tablespoons balsamic vinegar
2   tablespoons fresh lemon juice
¾   teaspoon salt
¼   teaspoon freshly ground pepper

Peel eggplant and cut into bite-size pieces.

In steamer basket over boiling water, cook eggplant, covered, until tender, about 5 minutes. Drain; place in large non-metal bowl.

In 2-quart saucepan over medium heat, blanch onions in boiling water to cover for 1 minute. Drain; rinse under cold running water and peel.

Place onions in bowl with eggplant and add tomatoes, basil, oil, vinegars, lemon juice, salt and pepper. Toss lightly.

Cover and refrigerate, stirring occasionally, to blend flavors, for at least 2 hours.

Serve chilled.

VEAL AND PORK SAUSAGE IN BOILED ONION CASINGS

Recommended Wine: Zinfandel

6 SERVINGS

6   large onions, unpeeled
3   cloves garlic, minced
½   cup mushrooms, sliced
3   tablespoons olive oil
¼   pound lean pork sirloin, cut into cubes
¾   pound ground veal
½   teaspoon fennel seed
½   teaspoon dried rosemary, crumbled
¼   teaspoon dried crushed red pepper flakes
¾   teaspoon salt
1   cup chopped fresh parsley
2   eggs
½   cup heavy cream

Bring 4 quarts water to boil over high heat in 6-quart stockpot. Add onions and return to a boil. Cook until onions are tender when pierced with a sharp knife, about 30 minutes.

Drain; plunge into cold water; drain again.

Preheat oven to 375 degrees. Lightly oil a shallow 3-quart baking dish.

With a sharp knife, cut a 1½-inch circle into root end of each onion. Scoop out the centers, leaving a sturdy shell. Repeat with remaining onions.

Arrange onions, cut side up, in

prepared baking dish; set aside.

In a large skillet over medium-high heat, sauté garlic and mushrooms in oil for 1 minute. Add pork, veal, fennel seed, rosemary, red pepper and salt. Cook, stirring frequently, until meat is no longer pink, 5 to 7 minutes.

Transfer meat mixture to food processor fitted with metal blade. Add parsley, eggs and cream. Process until smooth, about 1 minute. Spoon meat mixture evenly into onions.

Cut parchment circles to cover sausage mixture in onions. Butter parchment circles and place over sausage.

Pour ¼ inch boiling water in bottom of baking dish. Wrap dish tightly with aluminum foil and bake for 30 minutes.

Remove parchment circles and serve hot.

SMITHFIELD BUTTERFLIED HAM STEAK

Recommended Wine: Merlot

6 SERVINGS

6	*slices Smithfield ham, each about 8 ounces and cut ¾-inch thick*
8	*tablespoons unsalted butter*
1	*cup chopped onion*
1¼	*cups chopped celery*
2	*tablespoons minced fresh sage*
1	*teaspoon ground coriander*
3	*cups dry cornbread cubes*
½	*cup dry white wine*
2	*tablespoons all-purpose flour*
2	*cups apple cider*

Preheat oven to 375 degrees. Lightly butter a baking dish large enough to hold ham in a single layer.

Butterfly ham steaks. Using a sharp knife and holding it parallel to cutting surface, cut steaks crosswise, but not quite through, so meat forms a pocket and opens like a book.

In large skillet over medium-high heat, sauté ham steaks in 4 tablespoons butter until lightly browned on both sides. Transfer steaks to prepared baking dish.

In same skillet, melt remaining 4 tablespoons butter over medium heat. Sauté onion and celery until soft, about 10 minutes. Stir in sage and coriander.

Place cornbread cubes in medium bowl. Add sautéed mixture and stir in wine. Toss well.

Dividing evenly, loosely stuff butterflied ham steaks with stuffing. Secure with toothpicks.

Cover and bake until heated through, about 20 minutes.

Remove ham and keep warm. Stir flour into pan drippings. Cook over medium heat until browned. Gradually blend in cider and bring to a boil. Reduce heat to low and simmer until thickened, 6 to 7 minutes.

To serve, spoon hot cider sauce over baked ham steaks.

SOFT-SHELL CRABS

Recommended Wine: Chardonnay

6 SERVINGS

¼   cup all-purpose flour
½   teaspoon salt
¼   teaspoon freshly ground pepper
12   small soft-shell crabs, cleaned
½   cup unsalted butter
3   tablespoons olive oil
     Lemon wedges, for garnish

In pie plate, combine flour, salt and pepper. Dredge crabs in flour mixture, shaking off excess.

In a large skillet over medium-high heat, heat butter and oil. Add crabs and sauté until lightly browned on both sides, 5 to 6 minutes.

Serve hot, garnished with lemon wedges.

SAUTEED SHAD ROE

Recommended Wine: Semillon

6 SERVINGS

½   cup unsalted butter
¼   cup bacon fat
6   pairs shad roe (about 3 pounds total
     weight)
½   teaspoon salt
     Freshly ground pepper
     Lemon wedges, for garnish
     Chopped fresh parsley, for garnish

In large skillet over medium heat, melt butter and bacon fat. Sauté shad roe just until lightly browned on all sides.

Reduce heat to low, cover and cook for 10 minutes, turning frequently.

Season with salt and pepper and serve hot, garnished with lemon wedges and parsley.

PRECEDING OVERLEAF: Smithfield Butterflied Ham Steak makes the perfect centerpiece for a Maryland Sunday dinner.

OPPOSITE: Oyster Ravioli is an imaginative way to serve one of Chesapeake Bay's most celebrated denizens.

OYSTER RAVIOLI

Recommended Wine: Sauvignon Blanc

6 TO 8 SERVINGS

Ravioli Dough (recipe follows)
3 cloves garlic, minced
2 large shallots, minced
1 tablespoon grated fresh ginger
3 tablespoons olive oil
1 pint shucked extra-small oysters, drained

2 tablespoons chopped fresh fennel
2 ounces Bel Paese cheese, cubed
1/2 cup whole-milk ricotta cheese
1/2 teaspoon salt
1/4 teaspoon freshly ground pepper
3 quarts rich homemade chicken broth
  Red Pepper Sauce (recipe follows)

Prepare Ravioli Dough and set aside.

In large skillet over medium-high heat, sauté garlic, shallots and ginger in oil for 1 minute. Add oysters and fennel and cook, turning once, until oyster edges start to curl and become slightly firm, 2 to 3 minutes.

Transfer mixture to food processor fitted with metal blade. Add cheeses, salt and pepper. Process until smooth, about 15 seconds. (Or finely chop all ingredients and combine in medium bowl.)

On lightly floured surface, roll out Ravioli Dough into two 20 × 12-inch rectangles. With sharp knife cut dough into sixty 4 × 2-inch rectangles.

Spoon 2 teaspoonfuls of filling on one side of each piece of dough, reaching to within 1/4 inch of edges. Brush edges lightly with water. Fold dough over filling, bringing edges together, to form a square. With tines of fork, press edges to seal well. Place filled ravioli in a single layer on lightly floured surface. Repeat with remaining dough and filling, making 60 raviolis.

In 6-quart stockpot over high heat, bring chicken broth to a boil.

Add ravioli, return to a boil, stirring occasionally. Reduce heat and cook until tender, 5 minutes. Drain.

Serve hot, napped with Red Pepper Sauce.

RAVIOLI DOUGH

MAKES 1 POUND DOUGH

2¼ cups semolina flour
½ teaspoon salt
2 eggs, lightly beaten

1 egg yolk
1 tablespoon olive oil

Measure flour into mound on large wooden board and make well in center.

In small bowl, combine salt, eggs, egg yolk, ⅓ cup water and olive oil. Pour egg mixture into flour well and beat with fork. Continue beating egg mixture in circular motion to incorporate flour gradually into egg mixture, using one hand to support flour on sides of well. Use fingers to continue mixing until all flour is absorbed. Add more flour, if necessary, to make a dough that is soft but not sticky.

On lightly floured board, knead dough for 8 to 10 minutes. Divide dough in half and shape into 2 disks. Cover with plastic wrap and let rest for 15 minutes before rolling.

RED PEPPER SAUCE

MAKES 2 CUPS

3 large red bell peppers
1 large shallot, minced
1 tablespoon olive oil
¼ cup dry red wine
¼ cup rich homemade chicken broth
  Juice of ½ lemon
⅓ cup finely ground blanched almonds
  Salt
  Freshly ground pepper

Broil bell peppers 6 to 8 inches from heat, turning frequently, until skin is blistered and blackened on all sides. Transfer to paper or plastic bags, seal edges and let steam for 30 minutes.

Remove peppers from bags, discard peel, stem and seeds.

In blender, purée until smooth; set aside.

In small skillet over medium heat, sauté shallots in oil for 30 seconds. Add wine, broth and lemon juice and bring to a boil. Boil until reduced to ⅓ cup.

Add red pepper purée and almonds. Cook until thickened, 5 to 7 minutes.

Season to taste wth salt and pepper. Serve hot with Oyster Ravioli.

DUTCH PANCAKE WITH CHERRY CHUTNEY AND BLACK WALNUTS

Recommended Wine: Late Harvest White Riesling

6 TO 8 SERVINGS

6   eggs
1   cup heavy cream
½   cup all-purpose flour
2   tablespoons honey
½   teaspoon salt
2   teaspoons almond-flavored liqueur
         (such as Amaretto)
3   tablespoons unsalted butter
     Cherry Chutney (recipe follows)
½   cup black walnuts

Preheat oven to 450 degrees.

In large bowl, beat together eggs, cream, flour, honey, salt and liqueur with electric mixer at medium speed until smooth.

Place butter in large ovenproof skillet and set in hot oven to melt. Swirl skillet so butter covers bottom and sides; do not allow to burn.

Pour egg mixture into hot skillet and bake on second lowest rack for 6 minutes.

Reduce heat to 375 degrees and bake until pancake is cooked through and puffed, 5 to 6 minutes longer.

Serve immediately, with Cherry Chutney and garnish with black walnuts.

CHERRY CHUTNEY

MAKES 3 CUPS CHUTNEY

3   pounds dark sweet cherries, pitted
⅔   cup cider vinegar
½   cup honey
4   cloves garlic, minced
2   tablespoons minced fresh ginger
1   to 3 dried red chile peppers
½   teaspoon salt
½   cup seedless raisins
1   lemon, thinly sliced
1   teaspoon whole allspice
1   teaspoon whole coriander seed
1   teaspoon whole yellow mustard seed

In large 3-quart saucepan over medium-high heat, combine cherries, vinegar, honey, garlic, ginger, chiles, salt, raisins and lemon. Bring to a boil, stirring frequently.

Place allspice, coriander and mustard seeds on a 5-inch square of three thicknesses of cheesecloth. Gather the four points of the squares together and tie securely with string. Add to cherry mixture.

Simmer mixture over low heat for 30 minutes.

Remove cheesecloth bag. Serve warm, with Dutch Pancake.

The oversized Dutch Pancake can be served with a variety of sweet fillings, such as strawberries and rhubarb, as shown, or Cherry Chutney, as in the recipe above.

CHEESECAKE

6 TO 8 SERVINGS

1¼ cups graham cracker crumbs
2   tablespoons unsalted butter, at room
      temperature
½   cup plus 2 tablespoons sugar
9   ounces cream cheese, at room
      temperature
2   eggs
1   teaspoon vanilla extract
1   cup sour cream
      Fresh or frozen blueberries, for garnish

Preheat oven to 325 degrees.

In small bowl, combine crumbs, butter and 2 tablespoons sugar. Beat with electric mixer at low speed until blended.

Press crumb mixture into bottom and up sides of 8-inch round baking pan.

In large bowl, beat cream cheese at medium speed until smooth. Add ¼ cup sugar, eggs and ½ teaspoon vanilla and beat until light and fluffy, about 3 minutes.

Pour cheese mixture into crumb crust.

Bake just until top is set, 15 to 20 minutes.

Remove from oven and cool on wire rack for 15 minutes.

Increase oven temperature to 375 degrees.

In medium bowl, beat sour cream, remaining ¼ cup sugar and ½ teaspoon vanilla until combined. Spread on top of cake.

Bake until top is set, about 10 minutes.

Remove cheesecake from oven and cool on wire rack.

Cover and refrigerate overnight. To serve, garnish with blueberries.

BAKED APPLES

Recommended Wine: Muscat Canelli

6 SERVINGS

      Pastry Dough (recipe follows)
      Baking Sauce (recipe follows)
6   medium-size tart apples
1   tablespoon fresh lemon juice
½   cup sugar
1   teaspoon ground cinnamon
1   tablespoon unsalted butter
      Crème fraîche

Prepare Pastry Dough and Baking Sauce; set aside.

Preheat oven to 425 degrees.

Pare and core apples; sprinkle with lemon juice.

In small bowl, combine sugar and cinnamon.

Roll out dough on lightly floured

surface into three 14 × 7-inch rectangles. Cut into six 7-inch squares.

Place one apple on each pastry square. Stuff apples with sugar-cinnamon mixture. Dot each apple with ½ teaspoon butter.

Gather the four points of each pastry square up over apple. Overlap edges and seal.

Roll out dough scraps and cut out twelve leaf shapes. Moisten with water and place on pastry covered apples.

Transfer apples to 13 × 9 × 2-inch baking dish. Pour hot Baking Sauce into bottom of baking dish.

Bake until golden brown, 40 to 45 minutes.

Serve hot with crème fraîche.

PASTRY DOUGH

MAKES THREE 9-INCH SINGLE CRUST PIE SHELLS

3⅓   cups all-purpose flour
1   teaspoon salt
1¼   cups solid vegetable shortening, chilled
9   to 11 tablespoons ice water

Stir flour and salt together in large bowl. Cut in shortening with pastry blender or 2 knives until mixture resembles coarse meal.

Sprinkle 3 tablespoons ice water over flour mixture and mix lightly with fork. Continue adding ice water, a little at a time, until dough begins to stick together.

Divide dough into thirds. Press into balls, cover and refrigerate until ready to use.

BAKING SAUCE

MAKES 2½ CUPS SAUCE

1   cup sugar
3   tablespoons unsalted butter
½   teaspoon ground cinnamon
     Dash of freshly grated nutmeg

In small saucepan over high heat, combine sugar, butter, cinnamon and nutmeg with 2 cups water. Bring to a boil and cook until sugar dissolves, about 3 minutes.

Remove from heat and set aside.

THE
SOUTHWEST

RECIPES

Gulf Shrimp Piquant

Blue Corn Tortillas

Blue Corn Tortilla Soup

Grilled Barbecue Bread

Avocado, Grapefruit and Orange Salad

Rio Grande Vegetable Stuffed Peppers

Marinade for Beef Fajitas

Tex-Mex Marinade for Chicken Fajitas

Beef Fajitas and Tex-Mex Chicken Fajitas

Texas Chile Mole

Guacamole Southwest Style

Anaheim Red Chile Sauce

Green Tomatillo Salsa

Chorizo Stuffed Chile Rellenos

Gingered Peaches and Cream

Praline Kahlua Flan

Sopaipillas with Star Anise

One writer called it "a passion." Another referred to it as "plain stubbornness." Both were talking about one thing Southwesterners have in common—carefully preserving their traditions of regional cooking.

Few regions in America are so deeply steeped in traditions and the faithful use of local ingredients as the Southwest. While California cuisine may include French goat's-milk cheese, Russian caviar, and Greek olives all in one dish, a classic Southwestern dish is made entirely from the abundance found in that part of the country—chiles, corn, tomatoes, limes, and chicken, for instance. It was once called the "first American cuisine," and San Francisco chef Jeremiah Tower described it as "glamorous but approachable food, reflecting the open air, the open spaces and the beautiful colors of the region."

Yet this cuisine defies accurate definition. Is it barbecued beef and red beans cooked over a chuckwagon campfire by cowboys? Or is it those nippy, chile-pepper-enhanced Mexican flavors from just across the border, which have spawned that hybrid version called Tex-Mex? And what of the Pueblo Indians grinding up piñon (pine nuts) and grilling wild game over a mesquite fire centuries ago? What crop was domestically grown here thousands of years ago? Maize—and in all colors, too, yielding the golden yellow corn breads and blue corn tortillas of today. Southern accents? You bet, for a bit of the South overlaps here, evident in the local affection for black-eyed peas and pecan pie. These contrasting components were integrated by exploration, the cuisine unified and broadened by change. For Southwestern cooking is indeed all these things. And it is much more.

Often these original cooking styles come together in one picante menu, the flavors and textures blending miraculously. Sometimes they are kept separate. And local cooks insist on fidelity to their own style. Cumin becomes a must for certain simmered meat dishes, for example, or only poblano chiles will do for plump stuffed chile rellenos. An enchilada specialty has always been made with longhorn Cheddar and not Monterey Jack, thank you, and chile powder must be freshly ground from bright red ristra chiles. An area bordering on northern Mexico traditionally serves tortillas made with flour, while others are accustomed to them made of corn. Soft tortillas or crisp? The debate goes on.

PRECEDING OVERLEAF: Although New Mexico is often thought of as a land of arid deserts and stony mountains, it supports a rich and varied agriculture.

ABOVE: Distinctive adobe architecture of Santa Fe, New Mexico.

Nowhere are opinions more diverse than deep in the heart of Texas. True Texas images are common: long-horns, ranches that take days to drive around, bar-becues for 300 or 400 folks, and mesquite grills. But that's only the surface. Controversy emerges as one travels beyond Dallas or Houston to the Gulf-edged east, the vast central part of the state, the Mexican-influenced south, and the fertile west. Hours can be spent deliberating the merits of mesquite or hickory for gently roasting ribs, the relative sweetness in barbecue sauce, or whether beans belong in chile.

Chile reigns supreme as the subject of fierce com-petitive cookoffs. Almost every region, city, or individ-ual cook has a strong opinion about its ingredients. An authentic chile is not made with store-bought chile powder but with freshly ground, dried chile peppers. The meat is chunky, and it is simmered long and slow. Beans are eaten on the *side*, not *in* the chile (although some folks pour the chile *over* the beans). True Texas chile makes strong men weep and weak men beg to be put out of their misery. Humorist Will Rogers judged a town by its chile.

But there's more to Texas than chile or barbecue. Even a Texan couldn't brag enough to describe the bounty of the state's fresh produce, meat on the hoof, and seafood. Sweet Texas pink grapefruit and cannon-ball-sized cantaloupes are legendary. But there are also oranges, honeydews, watermelons, and dark, sweet figs. You think Georgia has a corner on pecans? They grow them by the bushel in south Texas. And seafood? From the Gulf the fisherman's net hoists in red snap-per, redfish, shrimp, crab, and flounder. Trout, perch, and catfish swim the rivers and lakes, and oysters nestle along the rocky beaches.

How these diverse ingredients fit together depends on regional traditions nurtured by ethnic traditions that arrived by a circuitous route. The barbecue is a classic example. Originating in Latin America, barbecue seemed like a good idea to the conquering Spanish, who carried it with them into Mexico and then the Southwest. The more refined art of backyard barbecu-ing was not the point of the early Texas version. It was simply a practical matter of how to eat hot, rib-sticking

A horseman in the Sangre de Cristo Mountains of New Mexico sports some of the locally produced riding gear that help make the state's arts and crafts so widely renowned.

food on the trail when you were two days from the ranchhouse. That's when the trail cook served up great slabs of beef, slathered with his own special brand of throat-burning sauce, a mess of beans, and biscuits made in a cast-iron Dutch oven—all done over on an open fire! From there the barbecue went high society in some parts of Texas: our thirty-fifth president, Lyndon Baines Johnson, entertained many a visiting dignitary at the LBJ Ranch along the banks of the Peder-nales River over a barbecue, accompanied by his favorite black-eyed peas. As at any respectable Texas cookout, the menu usually consisted of pork back ribs, short beef ribs, chicken, sausages, brisket, and even suckling pig. At times even the exotic specialty is tossed in: remember Elizabeth Taylor fainting at the sight of calves' brains being offered on the outdoor buffet table in the Texas saga *Giant?*

LEFT: Hardy chickens scratch contentedly on a New Mexico farm.
RIGHT: An Indian woman poses with ears of corn and a string of chile peppers, two staples of Southwestern cooking.

And just when you've got the Texas style straight in your mind, along comes Fredericksburg, a little bit of Germany set deep in the heart of Texas. German immigrants settled here at the turn of the century and assimilated their style of cooking with that of the Southwest. Have you ever had sauerkraut mixed with hot chiles and chopped bell pepper? You will in Fredericksburg.

Perhaps the most famous Texas export in modern times has been Tex-Mex, a style of cooking that began in the western corner, where Mexico sort of sidles up to the Lone Star State. At first, a poor man's Mexican food, Tex-Mex evolved into a highly sophisticated style of fresh ingredients and exotic combinations for color and dramatic flair. It has spread far beyond its point of origin.

Santa Fe, once the colonial capital of the entire Southwest, is the classic example of the whole region. Mention a culture or nation that influenced the Southwest and it materializes in Santa Fe—Spanish, Mexican, Indian, settler. Nearby, the rich farmlands of New Mexico produce an abundance of corn, squash, and

A New Mexico farmer and his son walk to work between irrigation ditches.
Thanks to irrigation, thousands of acres of desert land have been successfully cultivated.

tomatoes, as well as oranges, lemons, and Mexican limes. Thousands of acres are devoted to growing chile peppers alone, including the mild poblano, fiery little jalapeños, and serranos. Native cooks use fresh citrus to accent entrées, drinks, and desserts. Green tomatoes and flour tortillas reflect the influence of northern Mexico, where wheat is grown and used in place of the corn in tortillas.

Despite this horn of plenty and the importance attached to Santa Fe, the local cuisine actually remained Spartan until a few decades ago, when the area was discovered by writers, artists, and the tourists who followed in their wake. D. H. Lawrence and Georgia O'Keeffe, among others, were to draw international attention toward this one-remote country. Its peaceful isolation ended as the rest of the world learned of its attractions and its unusual style of cooking.

Along with the newcomers came something of a lusty frontier spirit, that true grit of founding something and sticking with it. And, yes, stubbornness, an unswerving dedication to tradition. That trait seems native to this vast region. Here, long before white people arrived, the Indians were foraging and subsisting on seasonal harvests of squash, melons, wild berries, plums, and avocados. Natives collected the piñon, to be used whole or ground into paste. They became experts at drying corn kernels, cooking them, and mashing them into a smooth paste for tortillas.

This was Pueblo cooking in its purest form. But it soon was to become embellished by centuries of exploration. Gradually, certain regional cuisines of the Southwest developed their own personalities, depending on which outside influence came first or stayed longest. It might have been the arrival of the Spanish,

the proximity to Mexico on the south, or Anglo-American influences to the west, north, and east. State boundaries do little to define the differences among styles of cuisine. It can only be ascribed to the sometimes-accidental happenings of history, the natural inheritance of a food-producing region, the spunky breed of people who came and stayed. And, oh yes, plain stubbornness.

TOP: *A Texas herdsman drives his sheep.*
ABOVE: *Two veteran Southwestern farmers bale hay.*

GULF SHRIMP PIQUANT

Recommended Wine: Fumé Blanc

10 APPETIZER SERVINGS

2   teaspoons dried red pepper flakes,
       crumbled
1½ teaspoons dried oregano, crumbled
½   small onion, chopped
2   cloves garlic, minced
3   pounds small Gulf shrimp
⅓   cup olive oil
½   cup red wine vinegar
½   cup dry vermouth
2   tablespoons paprika
¾   teaspoon salt
¼   to ½ teaspoon cayenne pepper
       Juice of 2 limes
1   green bell pepper, seeded and minced
12 green onions, including tops, minced
2   ribs celery, minced
2   cloves garlic, crushed
1   teaspoon dried oregano, crumbled

In 2-quart saucepan, bring about 3 cups water, red pepper flakes, oregano, onion and garlic to a boil over high heat. Add shrimp and reduce heat to low. Cook, stirring often, until shrimp are firm and pink, about 3 minutes.

Drain and rinse under cold running water. Remove shells and devein, if desired.

In medium bowl, combine shrimp with remaining ingredients. Cover and refrigerate 8 hours or overnight, stirring occasionally, to blend flavors.

Serve chilled.

BLUE CORN TORTILLAS

MAKES 6 TORTILLAS

½   cup stone-ground blue corn meal
¼   teaspoon salt
½   cup boiling water
1¼ cups all-purpose flour

In medium bowl, combine cornmeal, salt and boiling water. Let stand for 15 to 20 minutes.

Stir flour into cornmeal mixture to make a stiff dough. Turn dough onto a lightly floured surface and knead for 5 minutes. Cover and let rest for 5 minutes.

Divide dough into 6 equal pieces and shape into balls. On a lightly floured surface, roll out each ball into a 6-inch circle.

Place a small ungreased skillet over high heat. Cook tortillas, one at a time, for 2 minutes on each side. Keep warm until ready to serve.

The offshore waters of Texas provide the important raw material for Gulf Shrimp Piquant.

BLUE CORN TORTILLA SOUP

6 SERVINGS

3   large onions, chopped
2   red bell peppers, seeded and chopped
1   green bell pepper, seeded and chopped
10 to 12 cloves garlic, minced
2   tablespoons vegetable oil
2   quarts rich homemade chicken stock
1   cinnamon stick
1   teaspoon salt
1   tablespoon fresh cilantro, chopped
1/2 teaspoon ground cumin
1/4 teaspoon dried oregano, crumbled
    Vegetable oil for frying
6   Blue Corn Tortillas (recipe precedes)
    Sour cream and shredded Cheddar
        cheese for garnish, optional

In large Dutch oven, sauté onions, peppers and garlic in oil over medium heat until onions begin to brown, 10 to 12 minutes. Stir in chicken stock and simmer for 30 minutes.

Purée vegetable mixture in blender or food processor until smooth. Line a sieve with a double layer of dampened cheesecloth and strain; return soup to pan and discard vegetables. Add cinnamon stick, salt, cilantro, cumin and oregano. Simmer over medium-low heat for 30 minutes. Remove cinnamon stick.

Pour enough oil in 3-quart saucepan to measure 2 inches deep. Heat to 375 degrees. Meanwhile, cut tortillas into $1/2 \times 1$-inch-long strips. Fry, a few at a time, until lightly browned and crisp, about 1 minute. Remove with slotted spoon and drain on paper towels.

Divide fried tortillas between 6 bowls. Pour soup into bowls and garnish, if desired, with sour cream and shredded Cheddar cheese.

GRILLED BARBECUE BREAD

6 SERVINGS

1   2-pound loaf of thick crusted white
        bread
1/2 recipe Barbecue Sauce (recipe follows)

Cut bread into 2-inch-thick slices.

Brush both sides with Barbecue Sauce. Grill on barbecue grill over ash-covered coals until lightly toasted. Serve immediately.

OPPOSITE: *Blue Corn Tortilla Soup is a colorful and flavorful way to start a meal.*

AVOCADO, GRAPEFRUIT AND ORANGE SALAD

8 SERVINGS

3   *bunches watercress, thoroughly washed and dried*
     Juice of ½ lemon
2   *medium avocados, peeled, pitted and cut lengthwise into 8 thin wedges*
1   *grapefruit, peeled and sliced*
2   *large oranges, peeled and sliced*
1   *small red onion, chopped*
     Avocado-Mint Vinaigrette (recipe follows)

Tear watercress into bite-sized pieces and arrange on salad plates. Sprinkle lemon juice over avocados. Divide avocado, grapefruit and orange slices among 8 plates. Sprinkle each serving with red onion. Serve with Avocado-Mint Vinaigrette.

OVERLEAF: Avocado, Grapefruit and Orange Salad is a Southwestern specialty that reflects the region's ideal climate for fruits and vegetables.

AVOCADO-MINT VINAIGRETTE

MAKES 1 CUP

⅓ cup avocado oil
½ cup raspberry vinegar
¼ cup fresh mint leaves
¾ teaspoon salt

Place all ingredients in blender and process at medium speed until blended, about 30 seconds.

RIO GRANDE VEGETABLE STUFFED PEPPERS

6 SERVINGS

3 large green, red or yellow bell peppers
3 tablespoons chopped shallots
3 cups chopped mushrooms
2 tablespoons peanut oil
1 medium zucchini, shredded
1½ cups corn kernels, cut from 2 to 3 ears
½ teaspoon salt
¼ teaspoon freshly ground pepper
2 tablespoons dry sherry
½ cup toasted pecans

Preheat oven to 375 degrees.

In 5-quart Dutch oven, bring about 3 quarts water to a boil. Meanwhile, cut tops from peppers and discard stems, seeds and ribs. Parboil peppers, 4 to 5 minutes. Rinse under cold running water. Halve peppers lengthwise and invert to drain.

In large skillet, sauté shallots and mushrooms in peanut oil over medium-high heat until lightly browned. Arrange peppers close together, cut side up, in lightly oiled 9 × 9 × 2-inch baking dish. Divide mushroom mixture among peppers. Top with zucchini and corn. Sprinkle with salt, pepper and sherry. Cover and bake until heated through and corn is tender, 20 to 25 minutes. Serve, sprinkled with pecans.

BARBECUE SAUCE

MAKES 3 CUPS

3 cups ketchup
¾ cup Worcestershire sauce
¾ cup cider vinegar
¾ cup packed brown sugar
¾ cup unsalted butter

1 large onion, minced
1 large green bell pepper, seeded and minced
⅓ cup loosely packed fresh oregano, chopped

4   cloves garlic, crushed
1   tablespoon salt
1   tablespoon celery seed
1   tablespoon ground cumin
1½   teaspoons chile powder
1   teaspoon dried chile tepin, crushed
½   cup Marsala wine

In large Dutch oven, combine ketchup, Worcestershire sauce, vinegar, brown sugar, butter and 6 cups water. Bring to a boil over high heat. Add onion, green pepper, oregano, garlic, salt, celery seed, cumin, chile powder and chile tepin. Reduce heat to low and simmer, stirring frequently, until thickened, about 2 hours. Stir in Marsala. Cool and store in refrigerator for up to 2 weeks.

MARINADE FOR BEEF FAJITAS

2   cups dry red wine
¼   cup fresh lemon juice
1   green bell pepper, seeded and coarsely
        chopped
2   shallots, peeled
2   sprigs fresh oregano
1   tablespoon whole black peppercorns
1   teaspoon ground cumin
½   teaspoon salt
1½   pounds skirt or flank steak

In blender or food processor, combine wine, lemon juice, bell pepper, shallots, oregano, peppercorns, cumin and salt. Purée until smooth.

Trim outside layer of fat from steak. Place steak in glass baking dish or re-closable plastic bag. Pour marinade over steak and turn to coat. Cover dish or close bag and refrigerate, turning occasionally, for at least 8 hours or overnight.

TEX-MEX MARINADE FOR CHICKEN FAJITAS

2   whole skinless, boneless chicken breasts
1½   cups Tequila
¼   cup fresh lime juice
1   4-ounce can roasted chopped green chiles
2   to 4 dried serrano or jalapeño chiles
1   teaspoon ground cumin
2   tablespoons chopped cilantro

Place chicken in glass baking dish or re-closable plastic bag. Combine Tequila, lime juice, green chiles, dried chiles, cumin and cilantro. Pour over chicken; turn to coat. Cover dish or close bag and refrigerate, turning occasionally, for at least 8 hours or overnight.

OVERLEAF: Rio Grande Vegetable Stuffed Peppers includes corn and pecans, both long associated with the cuisine of the Southwest.

BEEF FAJITAS AND TEX-MEX CHICKEN FAJITAS

Recommended Wine: Merlot
8 SERVINGS

1   recipe Marinade for Beef Fajitas
1   recipe Tex-Mex Marinade for Chicken
     Fajitas
2   tablespoons vegetable oil (if pan frying,
     not grilling)
16   8-inch flour tortillas, warmed
     Green Tomatillo Salsa (recipe follows)
     Anaheim Red Chile Sauce (recipe
       follows)
     Guacamole Southwest Style (recipe
       follows)

After marinating, drain steak, reserving 1½ cups marinade for Anaheim Red Chile Sauce. Drain the chicken.

Prepare charcoal or gas grill. Grill skirt steak and chicken breasts 4 to 6 inches above heat to desired degree of doneness, turning frequently, 7 to 10 minutes. Slice beef and chicken across grain into strips. (If you wish to pan-fry beef and chicken, heat oil in large skillet and sauté quickly over medium-high heat to desired degree of doneness.)

Divide beef and chicken slices among tortillas, placing strips in center of each. Top with Green Tomatillo Salsa, Anaheim Red Chile Sauce and Guacamole Southwest Style. Roll-up to serve.

TEXAS CHILE MOLE

Recommended Wine: Zinfandel
8 SERVINGS

4   pounds top round of beef
2   pounds boneless pork shoulder
4   tablespoons lard
2   tablespoons corn oil
6   large cloves garlic, chopped
3   medium onions, chopped
1   green bell pepper, seeded and diced
1   tablespoon coriander seed
1   tablespoon crushed red pepper flakes
1   tablespoon paprika
2   tablespoons unsweetened cocoa powder

2   teaspoons celery seed
1   teaspoon salt
1   teaspoon ground cumin
½   teaspoon whole cloves
½   teaspoon dried oregano
2   pounds ripe tomatoes, peeled, seeded
     and diced
1   pound dried pinto beans
     Juice of 1 lime
1   pint sour cream

Trim extra fat from beef and pork. Cut into ¼-inch dice. In 6-quart nonreactive stockpot, heat 2 tablespoons lard over high heat. Add pork, in two batches, and brown until no longer pink, 8 to 10 minutes. Transfer with slotted spoon to colander and let drain.

Add remaining 2 tablespoons lard to pot and cook beef in small batches, draining and reserving drippings. Skim grease from drippings; discard grease but reserve broth. Set pork and beef aside.

Add corn oil to pot and stir in garlic, onions and pepper. Reduce heat to low, cover and cook, stirring frequently, until onions are soft, 8 to 10 minutes.

In food processor or blender, combine coriander seed, red pepper flakes, paprika, cocoa, celery seed, salt, cumin, cloves and oregano. Process until finely ground. Add tomatoes to pot and stir in spices and cooked meats. Cover and cook over low heat for 3 to 4 hours. Refrigerate overnight to blend flavors.

Next day, place beans in medium saucepan; add about 2 quarts water. Cover and bring to a boil over high heat. Reduce heat to low and simmer until beans are tender and water is absorbed, about 2 hours.

To serve, cook Texas Chile Mole over medium heat until heated through. Spoon over hot beans. Stir lime juice into sour cream and spoon a large dollop over each serving.

GUACAMOLE SOUTHWEST STYLE

MAKES 6 CUPS

4 *large avocados, peeled and pitted*
4 *medium tomatoes, seeded and chopped*
   Juice of ½ lemon
   Juice of 1 lime
⅓ *cup sour cream*
1 *small onion, minced*
1 *clove garlic, crushed*
¾ *teaspoon salt*
2 *tablespoons chopped cilantro*
¼ *teaspoon chile powder*
⅛ *teaspoon cayenne pepper*

Coarsely mash avocados in medium bowl. Stir in remaining ingredients. Cover and refrigerate until chilled, about 1 hour. Serve with Beef and Tex-Mex Chicken Fajitas.

ANAHEIM RED CHILE SAUCE

MAKES 3 CUPS

8 ounces dried red Anaheim chiles
1½ cups reserved beef marinade
1 teaspoon salt
1½ teaspoons dried oregano, crumbled
2 teaspoons ground cumin
2 teaspoons chile powder
2 tablespoons minced onion
1 clove garlic, crushed
¼ teaspoon ground cloves

Wash chiles under cold running water and remove and discard stems, seeds and ribs; drain. Place chiles and 2 cups water in blender or food processor and process at high speed until smooth.

Sieve mixture through wire strainer into small saucepan. Add remaining ingredients and simmer, stirring occasionally, over medium heat for 15 minutes. Serve hot with Beef and Tex-Mex Chicken Fajitas.

GREEN TOMATILLO SALSA

MAKES 1 CUP

1½ pounds fresh tomatillos, roasted, husked
     and chopped
6 jalapeño chiles, stemmed, seeded and
     chopped
2 bunches scallions, including green tops,
     chopped
1 bunch cilantro, chopped
   Juice of 1 lime
½ teaspoon salt

In a small bowl, combine tomatillos, chiles, scallions and cilantro. Stir in lime juice and salt. Prepare at least 1 hour before serving to blend flavors. Serve with Beef and Tex-Mex Chicken Fajitas.

Texas Chile Mole, served with homemade tortilla chips and a full-bodied red wine.

CHORIZO STUFFED CHILE RELLENOS

Recommended Wine: Zinfandel

6 SERVINGS

12   fresh Anaheim chiles
1   pound chorizo sausage, crumbled
1   medium onion, chopped
2   cloves garlic, crushed through a press
1/3   cup loosely packed cilantro, chopped
1/2   teaspoon ground cumin
6   ounces queso blanco (Mexican white cheese), cubed
5   egg whites, at room temperature
1/4   teaspoon cream of tartar
4   egg yolks
2   tablespoons beer, at room temperature
1/4   cup all-purpose flour
1/2   teaspoon salt
   Garlic Sauce (recipe follows)

Place chiles on foil-lined baking sheet. Broil 4 to 6 inches from heat, turning often, until skin is blackened and completely blistered all over, 8 to 10 minutes. Do not over-roast. Remove from heat and immediately close chiles in paper or plastic bag; let sweat for 30 minutes to loosen skins.

Peel peppers by holding under cold running water and scraping skin away with a knife. Cut off stems and remove seeds but leave chiles whole; set aside.

Preheat oven to 375 degrees.

Brown sausage in medium skillet over medium heat, about 10 minutes. Drain, reserving 1 tablespoon of drippings in skillet. Stir onion and garlic into drippings and sauté until lightly browned, about 10 minutes. Remove from heat and stir in cilantro, cumin, cheese and cooked sausage. Divide mixture and spoon into roasted chiles. Place in lightly greased 13 × 9 × 2-inch baking dish.

In mixing bowl, beat egg whites and cream of tartar at high speed until stiff but not dry; set aside. In small bowl, whisk together egg yolks, beer, flour and salt. Gently fold yolks into whites. Turn into baking dish and spread evenly over stuffed rellenos. Bake until lightly browned and puffed, about 30 minutes. Serve with Garlic Sauce.

GARLIC SAUCE FOR CHILE RELLENOS

2 CUPS

4   heads of garlic
2   to 3 tablespoons vegetable oil
2   tablespoons minced shallots

3   tablespoons unsalted butter
1   tablespoon all-purpose flour
2/3   cup sour cream

1 cup half-and-half
1 teaspoon salt
¼ teaspoon freshly ground white pepper
   Seeds of 1 pomegranate, for garnish

Preheat oven to 375 degrees.

Brush heads of garlic with vegetable oil. Place bulbs, flat side down, in small baking dish. Add enough water to reach ½-inch up the sides of the dish and bake, basting occasionally with oil, until very tender, about 45 minutes. Purée garlic through a food mill; discard skins and reserve purée.

In small saucepan, sauté shallots in butter over medium heat until soft. Add flour and cook, stirring constantly, for 3 minutes. Whisk in reserved garlic purée, sour cream, half-and-half, salt and pepper. Cook, stirring constantly, until mixture bubbles and thickens. Serve over baked Chile Rellenos, garnished with pomegranate seeds.

GINGERED PEACHES AND CREAM

Recommended Wine: Gewürztraminer
8 SERVINGS

1¼ cups sugar
4   egg whites, at room temperature
10 peaches, pared, halved and pitted
2   tablespoons hazelnut liqueur, such as
    Frangelico
2   tablespoons peach brandy
1   teaspoon minced fresh ginger
⅛ teaspoon ground cinnamon
2   cups heavy cream
    Fresh mint leaves, for garnish

In large saucepan, combine sugar and ¾ cup plus 2 tablespoons water over high heat. Cook, stirring frequently, until mixture reaches 240 degrees (soft ball stage) on a candy thermometer. Wash down sides of saucepan with a pastry brush dipped in cold water to remove undissolved sugar crystals.

In large mixing bowl, beat egg whites at high speed until stiff peaks form. Slowly add hot syrup in a steady stream to egg whites, beating constantly. Continue beating until mixture is cool and holds stiff peaks; set aside.

Coarsely chop 10 peach halves; set aside. In blender or food processor, combine remaining peaches, liqueur, brandy, ginger and cinnamon. Process at high speed until blended, about 1 minute.

In large mixing bowl, whip cream at high speed until stiff peaks form.

Gently fold ginger-peach purée into egg white mixture; then fold into whipped cream. Gently stir in reserved chopped peaches.

Spoon into eight 10- or 12-ounce dessert cups or stemmed glasses. Cover and refrigerate until chilled, 4 to 6 hours. Garnish with mint leaves.

PRALINE KAHLUA FLAN

8 TO 10 SERVINGS

4 ounces whole blanched almonds
1¼ cups sugar
½ teaspoon cream of tartar
5 whole eggs
3 egg yolks
2½ cups half-and-half
⅓ cup Kahlua liqueur
Whipped cream and toasted slivered
almonds, for garnish

Preheat oven to 350 degrees.

Spread almonds, in a single layer, in small baking dish. Bake, stirring occasionally, until golden brown, and toasted, 20 to 25 minutes. Remove from oven and set aside; reduce oven temperature to 325 degrees.

In large saucepan, heat sugar and ⅓ cup water over high heat until mixture boils. Cook, stirring constantly, until sugar dissolves. Allow syrup to boil, without stirring, until mixture turns dark brown. Stir in almonds and pour onto lightly greased foil-lined baking sheet. Allow mixture to cool.

Break almond praline into pieces and process in blender or food processor to a fine powder.

Put a kettle of water on to boil.

In blender, combine 2 cups of the almond praline powder with cream of tartar, whole eggs, egg yolks, half-and-half and Kahlua. Process at high speed until smooth, about 1 minute.

Place a lightly greased 10-inch quiche or flan dish in large roasting pan and set on oven rack. Pour egg mixture into quiche dish. Pour boiling water into roasting pan to reach 1-inch up the side of quiche dish.

Bake until a knife inserted near center comes out clean, 45 to 50 minutes. Remove from pan and serve warm or chilled. Garnish with whipped cream and toasted slivered almonds.

SOPAIPILLAS WITH STAR ANISE

6 SERVINGS

1½ cups all-purpose flour
2 teaspoons baking powder
¼ teaspoon salt
3 whole star anise

⅔ cup plus ¼ teaspoon sugar
3 tablespoons unsalted butter, chilled
Vegetable oil for frying
1 tablespoon ground cinnamon

Combine flour, baking powder, salt, star anise and ¼ teaspoon sugar in blender or food processor and process until star anise is coarsely chopped. Sieve flour mixture and discard large pieces of star anise.

In large bowl, cut butter into flour mixture with pastry blender or 2 knives until mixture resembles coarse crumbs. Add ½ cup water and stir to make a soft dough. Turn dough onto lightly floured surface and knead 1 to 2 minutes. Wrap dough in plastic wrap and let rest for 20 to 30 minutes.

Roll out dough on lightly floured surface into 6 × 9-inch rectangle, ³⁄₁₆-inch thick. Cut dough into 2¼-inch squares.

Pour 1½ to 2 inches vegetable oil in heavy large skillet and heat to 365 degrees. Add 3 to 4 rectangles of dough at a time and fry, turning once, until golden brown, about 2 minutes. Drain on paper towels.

Combine remaining ⅔ cup sugar with cinnamon and sift over fried sopaipillas. Serve immediately.

Almond praline and Kahlua, a Mexican coffee-flavored liqueur, make Praline Kahlua Flan a uniquely regional dessert.

CALIFORNIA

RECIPES

Sun Dried Tomato and Goat's Cheese Pizza

Almond-Topped Baked Brie

Cream of Artichoke Heart Soup

Fisherman's Wharf Cioppino

California Health Bread

San Francisco Sourdough Bread

Nasturtium and Watercress Salad

Springtime Asparagus Salad

Tree Oyster Salad

Stir-Fried Asparagus

Zucchini Herb Sauté

Roast Rack of Lamb with Sauce Paloise

Gilroy Garlic Chicken

Tomato Fettucini with Pesto

Sacramento Stuffed Steak

Lobster Tortellini with Chanterelle Sauce

Grilled Fig-Glazed Duck Breasts

California Fruit Tartlets

Kiwi Fruit Poppy Seed Cake

Early in the summer of 1934 Gertrude Stein and her companion Alice B. Toklas worried about whether they should depart their beloved Paris to visit the United States, where Miss Stein was to give a lecture tour. What concerned them most, Miss Toklas later related in her cookbook, was what sort of food would confront them.

As it turned out, both the tour and the cuisine along the way were immensely successful and gave the two women a whirlwind view of regional American cooking. It was in California, however, that their fears were truly allayed, and they began referring to the state as "God's Country." Throughout the Golden State they exulted over lush gardens, orchards, and olive and orange groves, and they became wide-eyed over their first avocado tree and the pyramids of the fruit stacked for sale. They delighted over the fields of artichokes near Monterey and their first taste of tender abalone at the old Del Monte Lodge. They purchased enormous crabs cooked on Fisherman's Wharf in San Francisco and enjoyed deliciously cooked sand dabs fresh from the Pacific Ocean. "Sun and a fertile soil," Miss Toklas was to write of California in her autobiographical cookbook, "breed generosity and gentleness, amiability and appreciation. It was abundantly satisfying."

Miss Stein and Miss Toklas were neither the first nor the last to note the abundance of California's great gifts from sea and land. The state has lured generations of explorers, missionaries, immigrants, gold seekers, and footloose chefs to share in its agriculture and culinary abundance. And the invasion has never stopped, even in modern times.

But, as some writers have indicated, all this great bounty was not entirely a natural gift. The gentle land and climate were there all along, to be sure. And the fish certainly swam in the sea, unhindered only by a few contented natives living by the shore. Yet it took outsiders to introduce the raw ingredients that now flourish in vast farms and ranches, as well as ways to prepare this abundance, and thus give rise to the spirited cuisine of America's favored West Coast.

PRECEDING OVERLEAF: California boasts a spectacular and varied landscape of rocky coasts, snow-capped mountains, and endless golden fields.

ABOVE: The San Joaquin Valley—California's agricultural heartland.

California, blessed at the start with a natural environment to nurture this future endowment, was even more blessed by an intense interest on the part of the outside world. In the sixteenth and seventeenth centuries, Spain, Mexico, the United States, Russia, and England all sailed by, dropped in, and flirted with this friendly land of fertile valleys, seafood-rich seas and natural harbors. Few nations were oblivious to its beauty and resources.

They found a coastline peppered by bays and inlets, facing peninsulas and scattered offshore islands. San Francisco Bay, of course, was a real prize, for an entire fleet could hide inside its protected and often fog-shrouded gate. The climate was pleasant, if not downright tropical, and all one needed to do was dip a net or a line and the table would be laden with wonderfully fresh seafood. No wonder the contented natives put up little resistance against the encroaching civilization. As one early explorer observed, why be ambitious when the best of everything was there for the taking?

The curtain rose on the first act of California's conquest with the arrival of Juan Rodriguez Cabrillo in 1542. He sailed into Pacific waters, searching for riches and power in the name of Spain. For hundreds of years afterward, California took on a definite Spanish/Mexican flavor.

We can thank the mission fathers for advancing and, in many cases, introducing modern agriculture in this new land. For, despite the commonly held belief that all of California was a Garden of Eden, many of the state's "indigenous" crops were not there at the beginning. In fact, at the time of the mission fathers' first settlements, the local Indians, Mexicans, and Spaniards, when not feasting on fish, existed mainly on

acorns, which were ground and made into bread or gruel.

The gentle friars brought European olives, dates, pistachios, and fig cuttings to this ideal climate. Perhaps their greatest contribution was the sweet raisin—and their most enduring, wine. So intense was the viticultural activity of the Franciscan fathers throughout California that the Spanish variety "Monica" came

Artichokes and grapes are two deservedly famous products of California's farms.

to be known as the "Mission grape." Father Junipero Serra first planted this deep black variety in San Diego de Alcala in 1769. From San Diego north to Sonoma, twenty-one Franciscan missions grew up along El Camino Real, each with its own vineyards.

Spain lost Mexico in 1821, and with it, California. In 1846 adventurer John C. Frémont helped to stage the Bear-Flag Revolt, pulling California away from Mex-

ican rule and leading it to join the Union in 1850. But the parade of eager visitors was not to cease.

When the lusty shout of "gold!" resounded in 1849, California was to become the fabled destination of every fortune seeker, not only from the Union but from Europe and Asia as well, and the influx of Italians, French, and Chinese would heavily influence the cooking styles of the state. Later came Finns, Czechs,

The gold rush of 1849 turned San Francisco into a metropolis overnight, with hopeful immigrants pouring in from all parts of the world. Its diverse ethnic heritage makes San Francisco one of the nation's most cosmopolitan and exciting culinary capitals.

Germans, and Hungarians; Basque sheepherders joined the list when the government imported them to tend flocks in the hills of the northern parts of the state. The mark they left is indelible even today. Italians found California's coast and inland waters rich with salmon, sturgeon, sole, cod, crab, bay shrimp, Pacific snapper, and one of the most prized of all—the buttery and tender abalone. The wharfs at San Francisco, and to a lesser extent at Monterey, were showcases for what could be done to prepare this profusion. *Cioppino*, the tomato-rich Italian version of bouillabaisse, found its second home and provided a natural match for San Francisco's crusty sourdough bread.

Their pockets filled with raw gold, the dusty, high-rolling gold seekers were hungry for luxuries and something better than the greasy stews and salt pork served up in the local boardinghouses. Oysters—even oysters from far away—became a coveted item. Soon sailing ships laden with the tiny prized Olympia oysters from Puget Sound were sailing south to San Francisco, where they were often paid for in gold dust. These delicate bivalves were responsible for one of California's most famous early dishes—Hangtown Fry. Hangtown really was a town—Placerville today—when a young prisoner requested something for his last dinner that he figured would be so hard to find it might stave off the rope scheduled for the following morning. He ordered up oysters and eggs. The young man's suspicions proved true, and he vanished before the bivalves arrived from San Francisco. The unflappable Californians cooked the oysters and eggs anyway, combining them into a culinary legend.

No one need entertain thoughts that grand dining wasn't important in the heady days following the stam-

pede for gold. Consider the gentlemen of the San Francisco's Chit Chat Club, which, up to the great earthquake and fire in 1906, had met monthly without fail for some thirty years to hear a paper read and enjoy a feast. The month of the catastrophe, as San Francisco lay smoldering, the determined members improvised an outdoor kitchen to prepare their meal and ate in the bedroom of the remains of a home. No one recalls the

A flower farm near Oxnard, California.

subject of the paper at all, but the meal was fondly recorded: oysters on the half shell for an appetizer, crab *à la poulette* for an entrée, Roman punch, dessert, and coffee. San Francisco, with its lusty and bawdy past, had come of culinary age and began setting the tone for the rest of the West Coast.

Today, California sets the pace for much of the nation. Perhaps it is, as one writer said, because California

offers the opportunity to create the best. It is no surprise that hot tubs, barbecues, tanning salons, and surfing fashions were born in this blessed landscape. According to M.F.K. Fisher, the lyrical writer who eventually settled in Sonoma County's countryside, California offers readily available fresh foods, interesting ethnic influences, and a desire for what is natural and healthy.

This perhaps explains the imaginative approach to modern-day cuisine in the Golden State, where limits and restrictions in combining ingredients have been left far behind in the wake of what is now called California cuisine. An impressive array of innovative chefs have passed through California's culinary history—Alice Waters, Wolfgang Puck, Jeremiah Tower, Barbara Tropp. These are not just local celebrity chefs but world-renowned artists who have influenced an entire nation. They have left their mark by adapting Old World dishes to New World ingredients: imaginative blends like ravioli stuffed with lobster, or a fresh salad of tree oyster mushrooms and toasted pine nuts dressed with a combination of walnut, hazelnut, and olive oils mixed with a Cabernet Sauvignon wine vinegar. Szechwan peanut sauce over oysters, warm goat cheese in a salad, roast duck with California figs. The brilliance never stops.

Perhaps the spirit of those early adventurers still lurks in the kitchens of California, resulting in a wonderful and eclectic mix of ethnic styles and home-grown ingredients blended by Western creativity.

A harvest of succulent California tomatoes.

The state's bounty is reflected in this distinctively California-style Pizza.

SUN-DRIED TOMATO AND GOAT CHEESE PIZZA

Recommended Wine: Zinfandel

10 APPETIZER SERVINGS

1 package active dry yeast
¼ teaspoon sugar
3⅓ cups all-purpose flour
1 teaspoon salt
⅓ cup plus 3 tablespoons olive oil
20 to 30 pieces sun-dried tomatoes in olive oil, drained
5 ounces fresh white goat cheese (such as California chèvre), crumbled
1¼ cups pitted ripe California olives, cut into wedges
⅔ cup chopped fresh basil
3 tablespoons minced fresh oregano or 1 tablespoon dried, crumbled
3 tablespoons capers
1 medium onion, thinly sliced
1 red or yellow bell pepper, seeded and cut into julienne
3 ounces fresh Chanterelle mushrooms, sliced
⅓ cup yellow cornmeal

Combine ⅓ cup lukewarm water (110° to 115°), yeast and sugar in small bowl. Stir to dissolve yeast. Set aside until bubbly, about 5 minutes.

Measure flour and salt into large mixing bowl.

Stir 3 tablespoons oil into yeast mixture; add to flour mixture along with ⅔ cup lukewarm water. Mix, adding additional water if necessary, until mixture forms moderately stiff dough.

Turn dough onto lightly floured surface. Knead until smooth and satiny, 8 to 10 minutes. Shape into ball. Place in lightly greased bowl, turning to grease all sides. Cover and let rise in warm place until doubled in bulk, about 1½ hours.

Preheat oven to 500 degrees.

Punch down dough. Divide into 10 equal pieces; shape each into a ball. Cover and let rest 10 minutes.

Flatten each ball of dough into 6-inch circle and form rim around edge of dough.

Brush each circle with remaining olive oil. Top each dough circle with 2 to 3 pieces sun-dried tomatoes, ½ ounce goat cheese, 2 tablespoons olives, 1 tablespoon fresh basil, 1 scant teaspoon each fresh oregano and capers and some of sliced onions, peppers and mushrooms.

Sprinkle cornmeal on 2 lightly greased baking sheets. Place 2 dough rounds on each sheet. Bake until golden brown and cheese is melted, 5 to 7 minutes. Repeat with remaining pizzas.

Serve immediately.

ALMOND-TOPPED BAKED BRIE

Recommended Wine: Sparkling Wine

10 SERVINGS

1   pound wheel of Brie, at room
        temperature
2   tablespoons unsalted butter, softened
½   cup sliced almonds
     Thinly sliced French bread

Preheat oven to 350 degrees.
    Place Brie in decorative baking dish with sides. Spread top with butter. Sprinkle with almonds.
    Bake until almonds are golden, 10 to 15 minutes.
    Serve immediately, with French bread slices.

CREAM OF ARTICHOKE HEART SOUP

Recommended Wine: Gewürztraminer

6 SERVINGS

8   artichokes
     Juice of 1 lemon
6   cups rich homemade chicken stock
¼   cup chopped fresh parsley
1   teaspoon curry powder
½   teaspoon salt
¼   teaspoon grated lemon zest
⅛   teaspoon freshly ground black pepper
     Dash of cayenne pepper
2   tablespoons unsalted butter, softened
2   tablespoons all-purpose flour
1   cup heavy cream
½   cup chopped shelled pistachios

Using small sharp knife, cut off stems and one-third of center top from artichokes. Bend back outer leaves, one at a time, and snap off from base of artichoke. Reserve for another use, if desired. Cut off top portion of leaves just below green tops. Trim off green areas on bottom. Cut lengthwise in half. Remove purple tipped leaves and fuzz; discard. Sprinkle cut sides with lemon juice; set aside.
    In 5-quart Dutch oven, bring 3 quarts water to a boil over high heat. Add artichoke hearts and cook until tender, 25 to 30 minutes. Drain.
    Purée hearts with 2 cups chicken stock in blender or food processor until smooth.
    Pour purée into large saucepan. Stir in remaining chicken stock, parsley, curry powder, salt, lemon zest, black pepper and cayenne. Bring to a boil over high heat.
    Reduce heat to low and simmer for 10 minutes.

In small bowl, blend butter and flour until smooth. Whisk butter mixture into soup, 1 teaspoon at a time, until smooth. Increase heat to high and cook, whisking constantly, until mixture bubbles and thickens. Stir in cream and cook for 1 minute.

Serve hot, garnished with pistachios.

FISHERMAN'S WHARF CIOPPINO

8 SERVINGS

2   large cloves garlic, minced
4   green onions, chopped
1/4   cup olive oil
1   large onion, chopped
1   large green bell pepper, seeded and chopped
1/2   pound mushrooms, sliced
2   ribs celery, chopped
1/4   cup chopped fresh parsley
1/4   cup chopped fresh basil
2   sprigs fresh oregano or 2 teaspoons dried oregano
1   bay leaf
2   large tomatoes, peeled, seeded and diced
1/4   cup tomato paste
3   cups Fish Stock (recipe follows)
1   cup dry white wine
1/2   teaspoon salt
1/4   teaspoon freshly ground pepper
1   pound (about 18) fresh small hard-shell clams, scrubbed
1/2   pound fresh rockfish fillets, cut into 2-inch pieces
1/2   pound fresh albacore or yellowfin tuna, cut into 2-inch pieces
1   pound medium-size raw shrimp, peeled and deveined
2   cooked spiny lobster tails, meat removed
1   pound cooked Dungeness or Rock crab legs
1/2   pound scallops

In 5-quart Dutch oven, sauté garlic and green onions in oil for 1 minute over medium heat. Add onion, bell pepper, mushrooms and celery. Cook, stirring frequently, until vegetables are tender, about 5 minutes.

Stir in parsley, basil, oregano, bay leaf, tomatoes, tomato paste, Fish Stock, wine, salt and pepper. Bring to a boil over high heat. Reduce heat to low, cover and simmer for 1 hour. Remove and discard oregano sprigs and bay leaf.

Add clams, rockfish and tuna. Cover and simmer for 5 minutes. Add shrimp, lobster and crab; simmer 3 minutes longer. Add scallops; simmer until shrimp turns pink and clams open, 2 to 3 minutes. Discard any clams that do not open.

Ladle cioppino into a tureen or serve in individual bowls.

OVERLEAF: *Fisherman's Wharf Cioppino proudly shows off California's abundant marine life.*

FISH STOCK

MAKES 2 QUARTS

1½ cups bottled clam juice
1 cup dry white wine
½ cup chopped fresh parsley
2 to 3 pounds raw fish bones and trimmings, cut into 4-inch pieces
1 large onion, quartered
2 ribs celery, chopped
1 large carrot, pared and chopped
2 slices lemon, including peel
1 bay leaf
½ teaspoon salt
¼ teaspoon freshly ground pepper

In 5-quart Dutch oven, bring 2 quarts water, clam juice, wine, parsley, fish bones, onion, celery, carrot, lemon, bay leaf, salt and pepper to a boil over high heat. Reduce heat to low, cover and simmer for 1 hour. Remove from heat; strain stock. Discard fish bones and vegetables.

Return stock to clean Dutch oven; bring to a boil over high heat and boil until stock is reduced to 2 quarts, about 15 minutes.

Store stock in refrigerator, or freeze. If refrigerating, reboil every 3 days to prevent spoilage.

CALIFORNIA HEALTH BREAD

MAKES 2 LOAVES

½ cup millet
2 packages active dry yeast
  Drop of honey plus 3 tablespoons honey
2 cups all-purpose flour
2 teaspoons salt
2 cups alfalfa sprouts
½ cup sunflower seeds
¼ cup safflower oil
3 cups whole wheat flour

In small saucepan, bring millet and 1½ cups water to a boil over high heat. Reduce heat to low, cover and simmer until millet is tender and all water is absorbed, about 15 minutes. Remove from heat and set aside to cool to room temperature.

In large mixing bowl, dissolve yeast and a drop of honey in 2 cups lukewarm water (110° to 115°F), stirring to dissolve yeast. Set aside until bubbly, about 5 minutes.

Beat all-purpose flour into yeast mixture until smooth, about 2 minutes with electric mixer at medium speed or 300 strokes by hand. Cover and let rise until doubled in bulk, about 30 minutes.

Beat in cooled millet, salt, sprouts, sunflower seeds, oil and remaining 3 tablespoons honey. Stir in whole wheat flour to make a stiff dough.

Turn dough onto a lightly floured

surface. Knead until smooth and elastic, 8 to 10 minutes, adding more whole wheat flour, if needed, to prevent dough from sticking.

Shape into ball and place in lightly greased bowl, turning to grease all sides. Cover and let rise in warm place until doubled in bulk, about 1 hour.

Punch down dough. Cover and let rise again in warm place until doubled in bulk, about 1 hour.

Punch down again; divide in half.

Shape each half into a loaf. Place in 2 greased 9 × 5-inch loaf pans. Cover loaves and let rise in warm place until doubled in bulk, about 1 hour.

Preheat oven to 350 degrees.

Bake loaves until richly browned and each loaf sounds hollow when lightly tapped with fingers, about 45 minutes.

Remove loaves to wire rack and allow to cool for 15 minutes before slicing.

SAN FRANCISCO SOURDOUGH BREAD

MAKES 1 LOAF

2   cups Sourdough Starter (recipe follows)
1   package active dry yeast
2   teaspoons salt
1   tablespoon olive oil
3½ to 4 cups all-purpose flour
3   tablespoons yellow cornmeal

In medium bowl, bring Sourdough Starter to room temperature.

In large mixing bowl, dissolve yeast in ¾ cup lukewarm water (110° to 115°F). Set aside until bubbly, about 5 minutes.

Stir in starter, salt, oil and enough flour to make a stiff but sticky dough.

Turn dough onto a lightly floured surface. Knead until smooth and satiny, 8 to 10 minutes, adding more flour, if needed, to prevent dough from sticking. Shape into ball and place in lightly greased bowl, turning to grease all sides. Cover and let rise in warm place until tripled in bulk, 2½ to 3 hours.

Punch down dough. Shape dough into smooth ball. Sprinkle cornmeal on lightly greased baking sheet and place dough on sheet. Cover and let rise in warm place until doubled in bulk, about 1 hour.

Preheat oven to 350 degrees.

Using sharp knife, cut crisscross pattern on top of loaf. Bake until light brown and loaf sounds hollow when lightly tapped with fingers, about 30 minutes.

Remove loaf to wire rack and allow to cool for 15 minutes before slicing.

SOURDOUGH STARTER

MAKES 4 CUPS

1   *package active dry yeast*
1   *tablespoon sugar*
3   *cups all-purpose flour*

In medium bowl, dissolve yeast and sugar in 2½ cups lukewarm water (110° to 115°F), stirring to dissolve yeast. Set aside until bubbly, about 5 minutes.

Gradually stir flour into yeast mixture and beat until smooth.

Pour starter into 6-cup glass or non-metal container; cover lightly with aluminum foil. Set in warm, draft-free place for 1 to 2 days; stir once or twice a day.

Cover and refrigerate until ready to use.

To keep starter fed and active, stir ½ cup all-purpose flour and ½ cup lukewarm water into starter every 5 days. Reserve at least 1 cup starter every time starter is used. Replace used starter with equal amounts of flour and water.

NASTURTIUM AND WATERCRESS SALAD

6 SERVINGS

8   *cups loosely packed watercress*
2   *medium-size purple or red bell peppers,*
         seeded and cut into julienne
3   *tablespoons olive oil*
2   *tablespoons fresh lemon juice*
¼   *teaspoon salt*
⅛   *teaspoon freshly ground pepper*
1   *cup small yellow tomatoes*
12   *to 18 nasturtium blossoms*

Wash and trim watercress, discarding any bruised leaves. Drain well and pat dry. Tear into bite-size pieces and place in large serving bowl with bell peppers.

Drizzle oil over watercress and toss gently until leaves are thoroughly coated. Add lemon juice, salt and pepper; toss again to mix well.

Arrange greens and peppers in 6 serving bowls. Garnish with yellow tomatoes and nasturtium blossoms. Serve immediately.

Nasturtium and Watercress Salad—as tasty as it is colorful.

SPRINGTIME ASPARAGUS SALAD

6 SERVINGS

2   pounds fresh asparagus
½   cup olive oil
3   tablespoons tarragon white wine
        vinegar
3   tablespoons minced fresh parsley
2   cloves garlic, minced
½   teaspoon salt
½   teaspoon freshly ground pepper
¼   teaspoon paprika
1½   teaspoons Dijon-style mustard
        Lettuce leaves, chilled
2   hard-cooked eggs, chopped

Wash asparagus; snap off and discard tough ends. Cut asparagus into 1-inch lengths.

In 3-quart saucepan, bring 2 cups water to a boil over high heat. Cook asparagus, covered, until crisp-tender, 1½ to 2 minutes. Drain. Place in large glass or non-metal bowl; set aside.

In medium bowl, whisk together oil, vinegar, parsley, garlic, salt, pepper, paprika and mustard until salt is dissolved. Pour over asparagus in bowl, toss lightly until well coated. Cover and refrigerate until chilled, stirring occasionally, about 2 hours.

To serve, tear lettuce into bite-size pieces; arrange on 6 salad plates. Spoon asparagus mixture evenly on top of greens and garnish with hard-cooked eggs. Serve immediately.

TREE OYSTER SALAD

MAKES 6 SERVINGS

1   large head radicchio, chilled
1   medium head romaine, chilled
¼   cup olive oil
¼   cup walnut oil
¼   cup hazelnut or vegetable oil
1   teaspoon Oriental sesame seed oil
1   teaspoon shredded fresh ginger
1   clove garlic, minced
1   large shallot, minced
1½   pounds fresh oyster mushrooms, sliced
½   pound fresh shiitake mushrooms, sliced
½   cup Cabernet Sauvignon or other red
        wine vinegar
1   teaspoon Dijon-style mustard
1   tablespoon fresh lime juice
½   teaspoon salt
¼   teaspoon freshly ground pepper

Wash and trim radicchio and romaine. Drain well and pat dry. Tear into bite-size pieces and place in large serving bowl.

In wok or large skillet, heat oils over high heat. Add ginger, garlic and shallot and sauté for 1 minute. Add mushrooms and sauté, stirring constantly, for 1 minute. With slotted spoon, spoon mixture on greens in serving bowl.

Stir vinegar, mustard, lime juice, salt and pepper into drippings in skillet. Bring to a boil and boil until mixture is reduced by one-third, about 3 minutes. Pour over mushrooms in bowl. To serve, arrange some greens and mushroom mixture on each salad plate. Serve immediately.

STIR-FRIED ASPARAGUS

6 SERVINGS

2½ to 3 pounds fresh asparagus
1 teaspoon Oriental sesame seed oil
2 tablespoons peanut oil
3 large cloves garlic, minced
1 tablespoon fresh lemon juice
2 tablespoons dark soy sauce
¼ cup slivered almonds

Wash asparagus; snap off and discard tough ends. Cut asparagus into 1-inch lengths; set aside.

In wok or large skillet, heat oils over high heat. Add garlic and stir-fry for 30 seconds. Add asparagus and stir-fry until bright green, about 1 minute. Stir in lemon juice and soy sauce. Cook, stirring constantly, until asparagus is crisp-tender, about 3 minutes total cooking time.

Serve hot, garnished with almonds.

ZUCCHINI HERB SAUTE

6 SERVINGS

12 baby zucchini
4 tablespoons unsalted butter, clarified (see Note)
3 small onions, quartered
1 teaspoon dried oregano, crumbled
1 cup loosely packed chopped fresh basil
¼ teaspoon salt
⅛ teaspoon freshly ground pepper
2 tablespoons dry white wine
2 medium tomatoes, sliced
⅓ cup shredded Monterey Jack cheese

Preheat broiler.

Slice zucchini lengthwise; set aside.

In large ovenproof skillet, melt butter over medium high heat. Add onions and oregano and sauté until onions are soft, about 3 minutes. Add zucchini, basil, salt, pepper and wine. Cook until zucchini turns bright green, about 2 minutes. Stir in tomatoes.

Sprinkle top of vegetables with cheese and broil 4 to 6 inches from heat until cheese melts, about 1 minute.

Serve hot.

NOTE: To clarify butter, melt butter in small saucepan over low heat without browning. Remove pan from heat and let stand 1 minute. Spoon off and discard any foam from top. Tilt pan slightly and spoon clear butter into small bowl, discarding milky solids.

ROAST RACK OF LAMB WITH SAUCE PALOISE

Recommended Wine: Cabernet Sauvignon

6 TO 8 SERVINGS

2   racks of lamb (each about 1¾ pounds
      and with 8 ribs), French trimmed
2   tablespoons vegetable oil
3   cloves garlic, minced
1   to 2 teaspoons dried rosemary,
      crumbled
      Sauce Paloise (recipe follows)

Preheat oven to 375 degrees.

Using sharp knife, score lamb fat in diamond pattern, cutting only ¼-inch deep.

In large skillet, heat oil over medium high heat. Add racks of lamb, one at a time, and sear fat until browned, about 1 minute.

Place meat, backbone side down, in roasting pan; rub garlic and rosemary into fat.

Roast until meat thermometer inserted in thickest part of meat reaches 140 degrees for rare, about 30 minutes, or 160 degrees for medium, about 40 minutes.

Transfer to heated platter; let meat stand for 5 minutes before carving.

To serve, cut lamb into rib portions. Arrange two ribs on each dinner plate. Pass Sauce Paloise separately.

SAUCE PALOISE

MAKES ABOUT ¾ CUP

⅓   cup dry vermouth
3   tablespoons raspberry vinegar
½   cup chopped fresh mint
6   black peppercorns, crushed
1   large shallot, minced
3   egg yolks
8   tablespoons unsalted butter, chilled
½   teaspoon salt
⅛   teaspoon paprika

In small saucepan, bring vermouth, vinegar, mint, peppercorns and shallot to a boil over medium high heat. Cook until liquid is reduced to 2 tablespoons. Strain liquid; discard mint, peppercorns and shallot.

In double-boiler, over hot, not boiling water, whisk together reduced liquid and egg yolks. Cook, whisking constantly, until slightly thickened. Add butter, about 2 tablespoons at a time, whisking constantly, until butter melts and mixture is thickened. Stir in salt and paprika.

Roast Rack of Lamb with Sauce Paloise—a special entrée for an elegant dinner party.

GILROY GARLIC CHICKEN

Recommended Wine: Johannisberg Riesling

6 SERVINGS

2   whole broiler-fryer chickens (each about 3 pounds)
1/3   cup chopped fresh sage
4   tangerines, peeled and chopped
40   cloves garlic, coarsely chopped plus 8 cloves garlic, minced
1/4   teaspoon salt
1/4   teaspoon freshly ground pepper
6   tablespoons unsalted butter, melted
1 1/2   cups half-and-half

Preheat oven to 350 degrees.

Rinse chickens inside and out and pat dry with paper towels.

In medium bowl, combine sage, tangerines, coarsely chopped garlic, salt and pepper; toss lightly. Dividing evenly, lightly stuff chickens with mixture; fold skin over opening.

Place chickens, breast side up, on a rack in a shallow roasting pan. Combine minced garlic and butter; brush on chicken.

Roast chickens, uncovered, basting 2 or 3 times, until juices run clear when thigh is pierced with a fork and the legs move easily when lifted and turned, about 1 1/4 hours.

Transfer chickens to warmed serving platter; keep warm. Remove stuffing mixture and purée until smooth. Press purée through fine sieve with back of spoon; discard solids.

In small saucepan, cook garlic purée and half-and-half over medium heat until hot, about 3 minutes.

To serve, carve breasts into slices, remove legs and wings; arrange on heated serving platter. Pass garlic sauce separately.

TOMATO FETTUCINI WITH PESTO

Recommended Wine: Semillon

6 SERVINGS

3   cups loosely packed fresh basil leaves
1/2   cup chopped fresh parsley
1/2   cup pine nuts
1/2   cup olive oil
1/4   cup unsalted butter, melted
4   cloves garlic
1/2   teaspoon salt
1/8   teaspoon freshly ground pepper
1/2   cup freshly grated Pecorino or Parmesan cheese
2   tablespoons vegetable oil
    Tomato Fettucini (recipe follows)

In blender or food processor, purée basil, parsley, pine nuts, olive oil, butter, garlic, salt and pepper, scraping down sides once or twice, until smooth. Pour mixture into medium bowl and stir in cheese; set aside.

Bring 4 quarts water and vegetable oil to a boil in a large stockpot over high heat. Add Tomato Fettucini and stir with wooden spoon until water returns to a boil. Cook just until noodles are cooked through, 45 to 60 seconds. Remove from water immediately and drain in colander.

Transfer pasta to large serving bowl and pour pesto over; toss lightly. Serve immediately.

TOMATO FETTUCINI

MAKES ABOUT 1¼ POUNDS

2½ to 3 cups all-purpose flour
4   eggs, lightly beaten
3   tablespoons tomato paste
1   tablespoon olive oil
½   teaspoon freshly ground pepper
¼   teaspoon salt
     Dash of freshly grated nutmeg

Measure flour into mound on large wooden board and make a well in center.

In blender or small bowl, beat together eggs, tomato paste, olive oil, pepper, salt and nutmeg until smooth.

Pour egg mixture in flour well and beat eggs with fork, using a circular motion, to incorporate flour gradually. Use fingers to continue mixing until all flour is absorbed. Add more flour, if necessary, to make a soft but not sticky dough.

On lightly floured surface, knead dough until smooth and satiny, 8 to 10 minutes. Divide dough in half and pat each half into a disk. Cover and let rest for 30 minutes.

On lightly floured surface, roll out each disk of dough into a very thin rectangle; dust with flour as necessary to keep dough from sticking. Starting at one short end, roll up dough jelly-roll style. Using a sharp knife, cut dough into ¼-inch widths. Separate strands and let dry until firm, about 1 hour.

Cook as directed in preceding recipe.

Sacramento Stuffed Steak—an unusual and flavorful dish from California's capital city.

SACRAMENTO STUFFED STEAK

Recommended Wine: Pinot Noir

6 SERVINGS

1   flank steak (about 2 pounds)
4   cloves garlic, crushed
½   teaspoon freshly ground pepper
2   cups chopped fresh spinach
1   cup chopped fresh sorrel
1   cup chopped fresh arugula (rocket)
½   cup fresh bread crumbs
1   cup chopped ripe pitted California
      olives
3   tablespoons minced onion
1   egg, well beaten
2   tablespoons olive oil
1   cup dry red wine
1   cup sour cream

Preheat oven to 375 degrees.

With meat mallet, pound steak ½ inch thick. Spread both sides with garlic and black pepper.

In steamer basket over boiling water, cook spinach, sorrel and arugula until just wilted, about 30 seconds. Transfer to medium bowl. Add bread crumbs, ½ cup olives, onion and egg. Toss lightly to combine well.

Spread spinach mixture evenly on one side of steak, leaving a 1-inch border. Starting with one of the longer sides, firmly roll up, jelly-roll style. Secure with small skewers and tie with string.

In large skillet over medium-high heat, brown meat on all sides in olive oil. Transfer, seam side down, to large roasting pan. Add wine, cover and bake until meat is tender, 1½ to 2 hours.

Arrange meat on warmed serving platter. Remove skewers and string.

Strain drippings from roasting pan into small saucepan. Stir in remaining ½ cup olives and sour cream. Cook, stirring, over low heat just until warmed; do not boil.

To serve, slice and arrange meat on heated serving platter. Pass sour cream sauce separately.

LOBSTER TORTELLINI WITH CHANTERELLE SAUCE

Recommended Wine: Chardonnay

6 SERVINGS

½ *pound cooked lobster, finely chopped*
1 *cup whole-milk ricotta cheese*
¼ *cup freshly grated Parmesan cheese*
3 *tablespoons fresh lime juice*
48 *round gyoza wrappers, 3½ inches in diameter (See Note)*
2 *tablespoons vegetable oil*
    Chanterelle Sauce (recipe follows)

In medium bowl, blend lobster, ricotta, Parmesan and lime juice until smooth. Place about 2 teaspoonsful of lobster mixture in middle of each gyoza wrapper. Moisten the edges with water and fold wrapper over filling to form a half circle. Press edges to seal. With finger on straight edge of semi-circle, bring 2 pointed edges together over finger; press to seal.

Place tortellini in a single layer on lightly floured surface; cover. Repeat with remaining wrappers and filling, making 48 tortellini in all. Let dry for 30 minutes.

Bring 4 quarts water and vegetable oil to a boil in large stockpot over high heat. Add tortellini and stir with wooden spoon until water returns to a boil. Cook until tender, about 5 minutes. Remove immediately and drain in colander.

Serve at once; pass Chanterelle Sauce separately.

NOTE: *Gyoza* wrappers are available in Oriental sections of food markets. If substituting egg roll skins for *gyoza*, use a floured 3½-inch cookie cutter or rim of glass to cut out 48 circles.

CHANTERELLE SAUCE

MAKES 5 CUPS

2 *cloves garlic, minced*
2 *green onions, minced*
3 *tablespoons avocado oil*
¾ *pound fresh Chanterelle mushrooms*
3 *cups rich homemade fish stock*

In large skillet, sauté garlic and onions in oil for 1 minute over medium heat. Add mushrooms and cook, stirring frequently, for 2 to 3 minutes. Stir in fish stock. Bring to a boil over high heat. Reduce heat to low, cover and simmer for 30 minutes.

GRILLED FIG-GLAZED DUCK BREASTS

Recommended Wine: Merlot

8 SERVINGS

2   *pounds fresh figs, chopped*
½   *pound fresh kumquats or oranges,*
       chopped
½   *cup chopped walnuts*
2   *cups dry red wine*
⅓   *cup honey*
¼   *cup light soy sauce*
2   *teaspoons dry mustard*
2   *teaspoons shredded fresh ginger root*
1   *teaspoon dried savory, crumbled*
½   *teaspoon celery seed*
⅛   *teaspoon ground cloves*
4   *whole duck breasts, skinned, boned and*
       split

In 3-quart saucepan, bring figs, kumquats, walnuts, wine, honey, soy sauce, mustard, ginger, savory, celery seed and cloves to a boil over high heat. Reduce heat to low. Simmer, uncovered, stirring often, until mixture thickens and fruit is tender, about 30 minutes.

Cover and refrigerate until chilled, about 2 hours.

Pour fruit mixture into a 13 × 9-inch glass or non-metal baking dish. Arrange duck in marinade, turning to coat. Cover and refrigerate for 30 to 45 minutes.

Prepare charcoal, gas or electric grill. Arrange duck breasts on grill 4 to 6 inches above heat. Grill until browned, 1 to 2 minutes. Brush duck with marinade and turn. Grill until rare, about 1 minute. Transfer grilled duck to heated serving platter; keep warm.

If preparing indoors, preheat oven broiler and broil duck breasts 6 to 8 inches from heat for 2 minutes. Brush with marinade and turn. Broil until rare, about 1 minute.

Return marinade to saucepan and bring to a boil over high heat. Cook and stir until mixture is reduced by one-third, about 5 minutes.

To serve, slice duck across grain; arrange on plates. Pass sauce separately.

OVERLEAF: California is one of the nation's largest fruit-growing states, and popular desserts such as California Fruit Tartlets make use of this incredible bounty.

CALIFORNIA FRUIT TARTLETS

Recommended Wine: Muscat Canelli

12 SERVINGS

Crème Patissière (recipe follows)
1¾ cups all-purpose flour
¾ cup powdered sugar
1 cup plus 1 tablespoon unsalted butter, softened
1 egg yolk
Fresh fruit such as peaches, kiwi fruit, strawberries, plums, apricots, mandarin oranges, blueberries, red raspberries, salmonberries, red seedless grapes and green grapes
½ cup apricot preserves

Prepare Crème Patissière; set aside to chill.

In medium bowl, combine flour, sugar, butter and egg yolk. Beat with electric mixer at low speed until mixture holds together. Press dough into ball. Wrap in plastic wrap and refrigerate until chilled, about 1 hour.

Preheat oven to 400 degrees.

On lightly floured surface, roll out dough ¼ inch thick. Using floured 4-inch cookie cutter or rim of bowl, cut out 12 circles of dough. Reroll and cut out scraps of dough.

Fit circles into 12 lightly floured 3-inch wide by 1¼-inch deep fluted tart pans, pressing firmly against sides. Trim edges even with top of pans; prick sides and bottom of each with fork.

Bake tartlets until golden brown, 10 to 12 minutes. Transfer tartlets to wire racks to cool to room temperature.

Peel and slice fruit as necessary.

Remove tartlets from pans. Spoon about 2 tablespoons Crème Patissière into each tart shell. Arrange fruit on top of Crème.

In small saucepan, melt preserves with 1 tablespoon water over medium heat; strain through sieve and discard solids. Allow to cool slightly.

Lightly brush glaze over fresh fruits. Refrigerate until chilled and glaze sets, about 30 minutes.

CREME PATISSIERE

MAKES ABOUT 1½ CUPS

6 tablespoons sugar
3 tablespoons all-purpose flour
¼ teaspoon salt
1 cup milk

3 egg yolks
1 tablespoon unsalted butter
¼ teaspoon almond extract

In small saucepan, combine sugar, flour and salt.

In small bowl, blend milk and egg yolks until smooth. Whisk about ⅓ cup of milk mixture into dry ingredients, making a smooth paste. Gradually whisk in remaining milk mixture.

Cook over medium heat, stirring constantly, until thick and bubbly. Boil, stirring constantly, for 1 minute. Remove from heat and stir in butter and almond extract.

Cover with plastic wrap placed directly over custard; refrigerate until thoroughly chilled, about 2 hours.

KIWI FRUIT POPPY SEED CAKE

Recommended Wine: Chenin Blanc

10 TO 12 SERVINGS

1¼ cups all-purpose flour
1½ cups sugar
⅛ teaspoon salt
6 eggs, separated
3 kiwi fruit, peeled and puréed
1 tablespoon poppy seeds
½ teaspoon cream of tartar

Preheat oven to 325 degrees.

In small bowl, combine flour, ⅓ cup sugar and salt; set aside.

In medium mixing bowl, beat egg yolks with electric mixer at high speed until thick and lemon-colored, about 3 minutes.

At medium speed, beat in kiwi fruit and poppy seeds until combined. Gradually beat in ⅔ cup sugar until sugar is dissolved.

At low speed, gradually add flour mixture, ¼ cup at a time, until

combined, 2 to 3 minutes; set aside.

Wash and dry beaters.

In large mixing bowl, beat egg whites and cream of tartar at high speed until foamy. Gradually beat in remaining ½ cup sugar, 1 tablespoon at a time, until sugar is dissolved and whites form glossy, stiff peaks.

Stir 1 cup of whites into kiwi fruit mixture. Fold kiwi fruit mixture into remaining whites.

Turn batter into ungreased 10-inch tube pan. Bake until top springs back when touched lightly with finger, 50 to 60 minutes.

Cool cake in pan suspended over funnel or bottleneck; about 1 hour. Loosen cake from pan with knife and gently transfer to serving platter.

Cut into slices to serve.

THE MIDWEST

RECIPES

Blueberry Flapjacks

Waffles

Rolled Oat-Zucchini Muffins

Chow Chow

Minnesota Pickled Salted Fish

Sesame-Caraway Flatbread

Smoked Trout Mousse

Cashew Soy Bread

Heartland Corn Chowder

Warm Bean Salad

Creamy Yellow Finnish Potatoes

Onion Rings

Barley-Corn Pilaf with Braised Fennel

Roast Stuffed Pork Tenderloin

Veal Cutlets with Berry Purée

Grilled Brook Trout and
Vegetable Kabobs with Lime-Dill Sauce

Peppered Steak Wellington

Bourbon-Glazed Roast Pheasant

Hazelnut Fudge Mousse

Hot Buttered Rum Apple Pie

They are America's heartland, their lakes and prairies decorating the country's chest like blue ribbons and gold medals from the Alleghenies to the Great Divide. Ohio, Indiana, Illinois, and Michigan. Wisconsin, Minnesota, and the twin blocks of the Dakotas. Nebraska and Kansas, Iowa and Missouri—their names resound with the strength of their early citizenry.

The Algonquin Indians gave Milwaukee its name, calling it "a gathering of rivers"; in 1844 Milwaukee's first German *biermeister* built his brewery here because its three rivers could provide enough ice for the cold storage required for his traditional lager.

The Chippewas named the whole region *Wees-kon-san*, which means "a gathering of waters"; Wisconsin's 15,000 lakes interlaced with a wonderland of meadows and pastures where immigrant Swiss cheesemakers could raise their Holsteins.

The Menominee named themselves after the "good grain" that modern Minnesotans call wild rice. Their early neighbors, the Winnebagos, may decline to be associated with their contemporary or motorized namesake, but they credit themselves with naming the hamlet of "Chicagu."

These days, on a summer afternoon, Chicago's Navy Pier is alive with nonstop festivals celebrating the multiethnic heritage of the Midwest. One week the pepper perfume of German bratwurst rides the air. A week later it's the aroma *robusta* of southern Italian cooking and *pancetta*. Another week it's Polish sausage, Belgian Booyah, or Bavarian *apfelkraut*. Or deep-dish Chicago-style pizza, its distinctive oregano scent reaching nearly to the Loop.

The recent revolution in American cuisine, however, has not been lost on the sensibilities of the Windy City. Old Town is now graced by a bumper crop of sophisticated, authentic bistros where the plate is the canvas and presentation is the art, their seafood often fresher than it is on either coast. It is no contest that "Chicagu" has become the culinary heartbeat of the heartland.

PRECEDING OVERLEAF: The golden wheat fields of South Dakota stretch to the horizon.

ABOVE: A tractor makes its way down the sleepy main street of an Iowa farm town.

Still, the gastronomic priorities of the Midwest have far more to do with tradition than with weight watching. It is not uncommon here for large families of large people to arrive at large German restaurants and feast on large servings of potato dumplings and red cabbage, smoked pork loin, hot potato salad with bacon dressing, creamed veal, spaetzle, hot sausages, pickled sauerbraten, liverwurst, cream of beer soup, sour rye bread, and cherry strudel with vanilla sauce—all chased by several rounds of good malted brew. "What I learned eating my way through Wisconsin," reports Betty Fussell, author of *I Hear America Cooking*, "is that . . . there's no status at all in being thin."

Thank goodness for that. Otherwise the richly larded Midwestern pantry would have been long since converted to an exercise room. But the culinary customs of first-wave German, French, Dutch, and Scandinavian immigrants that took hold in the mid-nineteenth century and then cross-pollinated with those of the later Italians, Poles, Czechs, and Greeks

Traditions die hard in Nebraska, where an old wagon stands at the ready.

still stand. Supported by the region's fertile soils and deeply underscored by its abundant wild game, fish, and plant life, the handiwork of these Old World farmers, brewers, bakers, and dairymen built the extraordinary framework of America's heartiest regional cuisine.

There were Michigan pie cherries, corn-fed Iowa beef and pork, milk-fed Wisconsin veal, Minnesota wild rice, hard and soft winter wheat from the Dakotas, and sweet Kansas corn. There were trout and whitefish, bass, muskellunges and several species of pike—gifts from the Great Lakes and the Ohio, Missouri, and Mississippi rivers and their tributaries.

Midwestern cooking is home cooking at its best. Good meats, simply seasoned. Rich stews, thick with the earthy muscle of root vegetables. Peppered rabbit, jellied veal, venison with cranberries, potato dumplings. Good soil and varied wildlife kept food on the table most of the year, but harsh winters demanded that the early settlers rely on the food preservation methods brought over from the old country.

Local boys help with the pumpkin harvest on a family farm in Wisconsin.

On German-American farms, cellars were full of sauerbraten—beef pickled in homemade fruit vinegars flavored with ginger, onion, and juniper—and sauer-kraut—cabbage merrily fermenting with apples and caraway. Fat rings of knackwurst hung cheek-by-jowl with beerwurst, the rich pork sausages that originated in Nuremberg; their heavy pepper and light mace seasonings gave forth a spicy holiday scent. Goose preserved with gooseberries and sugar kept a good three or four months.

Scandinavian fishermen pickled herring and smoked chub until they looked like gold leaf. Swiss dairy farm-ers made lovely cheese, including cream cheese and cottage cheese, whose subtleties far outstrip those of today's commercial attempts.

Brick cheese was a Wisconsin original, a German-Swiss variety, invented in Dodge County. Though de-veloped in New York to mimic German *Schlosskase*, Liederkranz cheese was produced in Van Wert, Ohio; its cousin, Old Heidelberg, made its New World home in Lena, Illinois. Prize-winning blue cheeses are still aged in caves near the Mississippi River in Nauvoo, Illinois, and Faribault, Minnesota.

And everybody baked pies—rhubarb in the spring; cherry, peach, and berry in the summer; apple and delicate green tomato in the fall. The dark aroma of sourdough rye bread was customary in German kitch-ens whose mistresses routinely made their own zwieback, stollen, and strudel. The French brought their brioches to St. Louis. The Danish brought their almond wedding cakes—their *Kransekage*—to Min-neapolis. The Italians brought their cannoli to Chi-cago. The Dutch brought their Christmas *Olle-bollen* to Cincinnati. Everybody used Midwestern wheat, but-

The straight, unbroken rows of corn on this Iowa farm have a simple, geometric beauty.

ter, and cream to their best advantage.

Naturally enough, this culinary bounty was and is the cause of much celebration. Michigan has its cherry festival. There's a popcorn festival in Indiana, a pumpkin festival in Illinois, a spike-rail cheese festival in Ohio, and Wisconsin's Door County is famous for its fish boils. County fairs throughout the region specialize in barbecued pork, corn on the cob swimming in local butter, cream puffs, and all manner of weiners.

But few Midwestern fêtes have as authentic an inspiration as Milwaukee's Oktoberfest, held around the Bavarian Inn in Old Heidelberg Park every September. Ooom-pah-pah bands belt out favorite polkas while men in lederhosen leap around the dance floor with petticoated, white-aproned matrons. Everywhere spitted piglets roast over open coals and 2-liter steins are continually emptied. A man in a Tyrolean hat suddenly stands and tearfully toasts his homeland. Everyone knows he means both Bavaria and the generous, fertile heart of America.

TOP: Harvest time in Iowa. Afterward, the celebration.
ABOVE: Newly harvested corn in a crib on a Galena, Illinois, farm.
OVERLEAF: The mighty Mississippi River—an apt symbol for the vitality of America's heartland.

BLUEBERRY FLAPJACKS

6 TO 8 SERVINGS

2   cups all-purpose flour
1   tablespoon plus 1 teaspoon baking
      powder
¼   teaspoon salt
1⅓ cups milk
¼   cup vegetable oil
2   tablespoons honey
2   eggs, lightly beaten
1½ cups fresh blueberries
      Butter and maple syrup, for serving

Preheat oven to 225 degrees.

In small bowl, combine flour, baking powder and salt.

In large bowl, whisk together milk, oil, honey and eggs until smooth. Add to flour mixture all at once and mix just enough to moisten flour. Fold in blueberries.

Heat griddle or large skillet over medium high heat. Brush lightly with oil. Using about ¼ cup batter for each, make a few flapjacks at a time. Cook until golden brown on bottom, about 2 minutes. Turn and cook 1 to 2 minutes longer.

Keep cooked flapjacks warm on ovenproof platter in warm oven while preparing remaining flapjacks.

To serve, spread flapjacks with butter and top with maple syrup.

WAFFLES

4 SERVINGS

½   cup all-purpose flour
½   cup whole wheat flour
1½ teaspoons baking powder
1   teaspoon baking soda
⅛   teaspoon salt
3   eggs, lightly beaten
2   cups sour cream
      Butter and maple syrup, for serving

Preheat waffle iron. Preheat oven to 225 degrees.

Meanwhile, in medium bowl, combine flours, baking powder, baking soda and salt.

In small bowl, mix eggs and sour cream. Add to flour mixture all at once and mix just enough to moisten flour.

Lightly oil waffle iron. Pour about 1 cup batter into center of lower half. Cover and bake according to manufacturer's directions.

Remove waffle carefully with fork. Keep cooked waffles warm on ovenproof platter in warm oven while preparing remaining waffles.

To serve, spread with butter and top with maple syrup.

PRECEDING OVERLEAF: A hearty breakfast of Blueberry Flapjacks or Waffles gears you up for a good morning's work.

ROLLED OAT-ZUCCHINI MUFFINS

MAKES 12 REGULAR OR 6 LARGE MUFFINS

2 cups rolled oats
2¼ cups all-purpose flour
2 teaspoons baking powder
¾ teaspoon baking soda
¼ teaspoon salt
3 eggs, lightly beaten
1½ cups buttermilk
¼ cup vegetable oil
⅓ cup packed light brown sugar
⅓ cup honey
1 teaspoon grated lemon zest
1 cup shredded zucchini

Preheat oven to 375 degrees.

In large bowl, combine oats, flour, baking powder, baking soda and salt.

In medium bowl, mix eggs, butter-milk, oil, brown sugar, honey and lemon zest until smooth. Stir in zucchini.

Add egg mixture all at once to oat mixture and mix just enough to moisten flour; batter will be lumpy. Spoon evenly into 12 greased- or paper-lined 2½-inch muffin cups or 6 greased 2-cup custard cups. Bake until golden brown, 18 to 20 minutes for regular size muffins and 25 to 30 minutes for large muffins.

Remove muffins from pan and cool on wire rack. Serve warm or at room temperature.

CHOW CHOW

MAKES 3 CUPS

1 pound zucchini, chopped
1 pound green tomatoes, chopped
1 large onion, chopped
2 green bell peppers, seeded and chopped
1 red bell pepper, seeded and chopped
2 teaspoons salt
1 cup cider vinegar
2 teaspoons grated fresh ginger root
3 cloves garlic, minced
2 tablespoons sugar
½ teaspoon dry mustard
½ teaspoon celery seed
¼ teaspoon turmeric
¼ teaspoon cayenne pepper

In large nonreactive bowl, combine zucchini, green tomatoes, onion and bell peppers. Sprinkle with salt; toss lightly. Cover and refrigerate for 3½ to 4 hours.

Drain vegetables; discard liquid.

In 3-quart saucepan, bring vegetables, vinegar, ginger, garlic, sugar, mustard, celery seed, turmeric and cayenne to a boil over high heat. Reduce heat to low and simmer until vegetables are tender, 25 to 30 minutes.

Remove from heat, cover and refrigerate until chilled, about 3 hours.

MINNESOTA PICKLED SALTED FISH

10 APPETIZER SERVINGS

2   *pounds salted fish fillets, such as
      walleyed pike, herring, trout or
      smelts*
1   *large onion, sliced*
3   *cloves garlic, sliced*
1   *tablespoon whole yellow mustard seed*
2   *tablespoons chopped fresh dill or 2
      teaspoons dried*
3   *tablespoons grated fresh horseradish*
2   *teaspoons grated fresh ginger root*
1   *teaspoon whole allspice berries*
3   *bay leaves*
1   *cup distilled white vinegar*
½   *cup sugar*

    TO SERVE:

½   *cup sour cream*
1   *cucumber, scored and sliced*
4   *beets, cooked, chilled, peeled and sliced*
2   *large carrots, pared and sliced*
1   *slice red onion
      Chopped hard-cooked eggs
      Sprigs of fresh dill
      Sesame-Caraway Flatbread (recipe
      follows)*

Four to 6 days before serving, freshen salted fish by rinsing well with cold water. Place in deep glass or stainless-steel bowl and add cold water to cover. Cover and refrigerate for 2 to 3 days, changing water 2 or 3 times a day and rinsing fish well at each change.

Cut fish fillets into 2-inch pieces. In 1-quart glass container with cover, layer some of fish, onion, garlic, mustard seed, dill, horseradish, ginger, allspice and bay leaves. Repeat with remaining ingredients.

In small saucepan, bring vinegar, sugar and ¾ cup water to a boil over high heat. Cook until sugar dissolves. Pour over layered fish mixture.

Cover and refrigerate for 2 to 3 days, stirring occasionally.

To serve, drain fish and discard marinade. Stir sour cream into 1 cup pickled fish; arrange in center of serving platter. Arrange remaining pickled fish around sour cream mixture. Garnish with cucumber, beets, carrots, purple onion, eggs and sprigs of dill. Serve chilled with Sesame-Caraway Flatbread.

SESAME-CARAWAY FLATBREAD

10 APPETIZER SERVINGS

1   *cup rye flour*
1   *cup whole wheat flour*
1   *tablespoon sesame seeds*
1   *teaspoon salt*

1   *teaspoon baking soda*
1   *teaspoon caraway seeds*
1   *cup buttermilk*
4   *tablespoons unsalted butter, melted*

Preheat oven to 350 degrees. Lightly grease several large baking sheets.

Combine rye and whole wheat flours, sesame seeds, salt, baking soda and caraway seeds in medium bowl. Stir in buttermilk and melted butter.

Turn dough onto lightly floured surface and knead until smooth, about 2 minutes. Add more whole wheat flour, if needed, to prevent dough from sticking.

Shape dough into cylinder; cut into 6 equal pieces. One at a time, roll out dough on lightly floured surface into 10-inch rounds, adding more flour, if needed. Transfer rounds to prepared baking sheets and prick surface evenly with fork.

Score each round with knife into 12 pie-shaped wedges.

Bake until firm and edges are browned, 10 to 12 minutes. Remove flatbread to wire rack to cool to room temperature.

Minnesota Pickled Salted Fish—a traditional appetizer from the state known as the Land of 10,000 Lakes.

SMOKED TROUT MOUSSE

Recommended Wine: Johannisberg Riesling

10 APPETIZER SERVINGS

1   envelope unflavored gelatin
½   cup boiling water
2   tablespoons minced shallots
½   pound fresh mushrooms, cleaned and
         finely chopped
2   tablespoons unsalted butter
4   ounces smoked trout, flaked
½   cup walnuts, lightly toasted
½   cup loosely packed fresh parsley
2   tablespoons fresh lemon juice
¼   teaspoon salt
⅛   teaspoon dried dill
⅛   teaspoon cayenne pepper
1   egg white
¼   teaspoon cream of tartar
1   cup heavy cream
         Raw vegetables and crisp crackers, for
           serving

In small bowl, soften gelatin in ¼ cup cold water. Add ½ cup boiling water and stir until gelatin dissolves. Set aside to cool to room temperature.

In medium skillet over medium-high heat, sauté shallots and mushrooms in butter until mushrooms are tender, 3 to 5 minutes.

Transfer to food processor fitted with metal blade. Add trout, walnuts, parsley, lemon juice, salt, dill and cayenne. Process until mixture is finely chopped, 5 to 10 seconds.

In small mixing bowl, beat egg white and cream of tartar with electric mixer at high speed until stiff peaks form; fold into gelatin mixture. Fold trout mixture into gelatin mixture.

In large mixing bowl, beat cream with electric mixer at high speed until stiff peaks form. Fold trout mixture into whipped cream.

Turn mixture into 6-cup serving bowl. Cover and refrigerate until set, about 4 hours. Mixture will be soft.

Serve with raw vegetables and crisp crackers.

CASHEW SOY BREAD

MAKES 2 LOAVES

2/3   cup soy flour
1   tablespoon sugar
1   package active dry yeast
1   cup milk
5½   to 6 cups all-purpose flour
1   cup finely chopped ground, roasted
     salted cashews
1/3   cup vegetable oil
2   teaspoons salt

In small skillet over medium high heat, toast soy flour, stirring frequently, until light brown, about 5 minutes; set aside.

In large mixing bowl, combine lukewarm water (110° to 115°F), sugar and yeast. Let stand until bubbly, about 5 minutes.

Meanwhile, heat milk with 1½ cups water in small saucepan over low heat until just warm. Stir into yeast mixture.

Add 2½ cups all-purpose flour to yeast mixture and beat with electric mixer at medium speed or 300 strokes by hand. Cover bowl and let rise in warm place until doubled in bulk, about 45 minutes.

Stir down dough and add toasted soy flour, cashews, oil, salt and enough additional remaining all-purpose flour to make a moderately stiff dough. Turn dough onto lightly floured surface and knead until smooth and satiny, 8 to 10 minutes.

Shape into ball and place in lightly greased bowl, turning to grease all sides. Cover and let rise in warm place until doubled in bulk, about 1½ hours.

Punch down dough; divide in half. Cover and let rest 10 minutes. Shape each half into a loaf. Place in two greased 9 × 5-inch loaf pans. Cover and let rise in warm place until doubled in bulk, about 1 hour.

Preheat oven to 350 degrees.

Bake until golden brown and loaves sound hollow when lightly tapped with fingers, about 45 minutes.

Remove loaves to wire rack and let cool for 15 minutes before slicing.

HEARTLAND CORN CHOWDER

Recommended Wine: Fumé Blanc

6 TO 8 SERVINGS

1	to 1¼ pounds smoked ham bones
3	medium onions, peeled and quartered
3	medium carrots, pared and quartered
3	medium potatoes, pared and quartered
4	ribs celery
1	green bell pepper, seeded and sliced
2	bay leaves
2	teaspoons dried thyme, crumbled
2	teaspoons dried tarragon, crumbled
1	teaspoon salt
¼	teaspoon freshly ground pepper
2	cups milk
4	cups fresh corn kernels, cut from 6 to 8 ears
8	slices bacon, cooked and crumbled

ABOVE AND OPPOSITE: *Farm-fresh produce makes Heartland Corn Chowder a robust Midwestern treat.*

In 5-quart Dutch oven, bring 3 quarts water, ham bones, onions, carrots, potatoes, celery, bell pepper, bay leaves, thyme, tarragon, salt and pepper to a boil over medium high heat. Reduce heat to low and simmer, partially covered, for 2½ to 3 hours.

Strain broth; discard bones and bay leaves. Skim off and discard fat from broth.

Purée vegetables in blender or food processor until smooth.

Return broth and puréed vegetables to Dutch oven. Add milk and corn. Bring to a simmer over medium high heat. Reduce heat to low and cook for 5 minutes without boiling.

Serve hot, garnished with crumbled bacon.

WARM BEAN SALAD

8 SERVINGS

1 cup dried soybeans
1 cup dried azuki or small red beans
1 cup dried lentils
¾ cup sunflower seed oil
½ cup malt or cider vinegar
2 cups chopped red onions
2 cups chopped fresh parsley
1½ cups chopped celery
2 tablespoons chopped fresh marjoram or
2 teaspoons dried
1 teaspoon salt
¼ teaspoon freshly ground pepper
Cherry tomatoes

Wash and sort all beans.

In 5-quart Dutch oven, bring 2 quarts cold water, soybeans and azuki beans to a boil over high heat. Boil for 2 minutes. Remove from heat, cover and let beans soak for 30 minutes. Drain beans and return to Dutch oven; discard liquid.

Add 2 quarts cold water to beans, cover and bring to a boil over high heat. Reduce heat to low. Simmer until beans are almost tender, about 1 hour.

Add lentils, cover and bring to a boil over high heat. Reduce heat to low, and simmer until beans and lentils are tender, about 30 minutes longer.

Drain beans and place in large serving bowl. Cover to keep warm.

In medium bowl, combine oil, vinegar, onions, parsley, celery, marjoram, salt and pepper until well blended.

Pour vinegar mixture over beans and toss until thoroughly mixed.

Serve hot or let cool to room temperature.

To serve, garnish with cherry tomatoes.

CREAMY YELLOW FINNISH POTATOES

6 SERVINGS

3 pounds yellow Finnish or white boiling
potatoes
2 cups heavy cream
Salt and freshly ground pepper

Preheat oven to 325 degrees.

Pare and cut potatoes into ¼-inch slices. Arrange potato slices in even, overlapping layers in 12 × 8-inch baking pan. Pour cream over potatoes.

Bake until potatoes are tender and creamy and top is crusty, 1½ to 1¾ hours.

To serve, season potatoes with salt and pepper after baking. (If salted before baking, the salt will separate the cream and the potatoes will not have a creamy texture.)

ONION RINGS

6 SERVINGS

1   to 2 quarts vegetable oil
3   large onions, peeled and sliced ¼ inch
      thick
1   cup all-purpose flour
2   tablespoons cornstarch
½   teaspoon baking powder
¼   teaspoon salt
1   egg, lightly beaten
1   cup milk

Pour 1 inch of oil into 3-quart saucepan and place over medium-high heat until it reaches 375 degrees.

Meanwhile, separate onion slices into rings. Place in large bowl and cover with ice water; set aside.

In medium bowl, combine flour, cornstarch, baking powder and salt.

In small bowl, beat together egg and milk until smooth. Add egg mixture all at once to flour mixture and mix enough to just moisten flour.

Drain onions; pat dry with paper towels. With fork, dip each onion slice in flour mixture, turning to coat completely.

Fry rings in a single layer in hot oil until golden, 2 to 3 minutes. Remove with slotted spoon or tongs and drain on paper towels.

Serve hot.

BARLEY-CORN PILAF WITH BRAISED FENNEL

6 SERVINGS

2   tablespoons unsalted butter
1½   cups pearl barley
1   quart rich homemade chicken stock or
        broth
½   teaspoon salt
¼   teaspoon freshly ground pepper
1   bulb fennel, trimmed and chopped
2   cups fresh corn kernels, cut from 4 to 5
        ears

In 3-quart saucepan, melt butter over medium heat. Add barley and cook, stirring often, until golden, about 5 minutes. Add broth, salt and pepper and bring to a boil. Reduce heat to low, cover and simmer 30 minutes.

Add fennel and cook 15 minutes. Add corn and cook until liquid is absorbed and fennel is tender, about 5 minutes.

Serve hot.

ROAST STUFFED PORK TENDERLOIN

Recommended Wine: Pinot Noir

6 TO 8 SERVINGS

²/₃ cup wild rice, washed
1 cup chopped celery
½ cup chopped onion
3 tablespoons chopped fresh mint
¼ to ½ teaspoon salt
⅛ to ¼ teaspoon freshly ground pepper
3 tablespoons unsalted butter
4 fresh plums, pitted and sliced
1 center cut boneless pork loin (about 3½ pounds)
3 tablespoons all-purpose flour
1 teaspoon dried rosemary, crumbled
½ teaspoon freshly grated ginger root
¼ teaspoon ground sage

In small saucepan, bring 2 cups water to a boil over high heat. Stir in rice, and reduce heat to low. Cover and simmer until rice is tender and all liquid is absorbed, 45 to 50 minutes. Transfer to medium bowl.

Preheat oven to 375 degrees.

In small skillet over medium-high heat, sauté celery, onion, mint, ¼ teaspoon salt and ⅛ teaspoon pepper in butter until vegetables are tender, about 5 minutes.

Add plums and stir mixture into rice. Toss lightly.

With long sharp knife, cut pork lengthwise, 1½-inches deep. Make another cut on each side of first cut so that meat will almost lay flat.

Spread rice mixture evenly over cut side of meat. Roll up to enclose filling. Tie meat securely with string. Place meat, cut side down, on rack in lightly greased, covered roasting pan.

Cover and bake until a meat thermometer inserted in thickest part of pork registers 170 degrees, 1½ to 2 hours.

Transfer to heated serving platter. Let stand for 15 minutes before carving.

Discard all but 3 tablespoons of pan drippings. Stir in flour and cook over low heat until thickened, 2 minutes.

Gradually whisk in 3 cups water. Add rosemary, ginger and sage. Increase heat to high and bring to a boil, stirring constantly. Reduce heat to low and simmer until bubbly and thickened, about 10 minutes. Season to taste with remaining salt and pepper.

To serve, remove strings from meat. Slice and arrange meat on heated serving platter. Pass gravy separately.

VEAL CUTLETS WITH BERRY PUREE

Recommended Wine: Merlot

6 SERVINGS

⅓   cup all-purpose flour
½   to 1 teaspoon salt
⅛   to ¼ teaspoon freshly ground pepper
¼   teaspoon dried rosemary, crumbled
1½   pounds veal cutlets, sliced ⅛ inch thick
3   to 5 tablespoons olive oil
3   tablespoons unsalted butter
3   cloves garlic, minced
1   large shallot, minced
⅔   cup chopped fresh chervil or parsley
¾   cup dry Marsala
1   cup fresh or frozen red raspberries
1   cup fresh or frozen blackberries
1   tablespoon fresh lemon juice
⅛   teaspoon freshly grated nutmeg
½   cup heavy cream
1   to 2 teaspoons finely grated lemon zest

Preheat oven to 250 degrees.

In shallow dish or plate, combine flour, ½ teaspoon salt, ⅛ teaspoon pepper and rosemary. Dredge meat in flour mixture and shake off excess.

In large skillet over medium heat, melt 3 tablespoons oil with butter. Brown veal on both sides, a few pieces at a time, 1 to 2 minutes.

Transfer meat to ovenproof serving platter and keep warm in oven.

Add remaining oil, if necessary, to skillet. Add garlic, shallot and ½ cup chopped chervil and sauté for 1 minute. Stir in Marsala, raspberries, black-berries, lemon juice and nutmeg. Increase heat to high and bring to a boil. Boil sauce, stirring frequently, until reduced by one-third, about 5 minutes.

Purée sauce in blender or food processor. Press purée through fine strainer into skillet; discard seeds.

Bring purée to a boil over high heat; stir in cream. Add remaining salt and pepper.

To serve, spoon berry purée on each serving plate and top with 2 or 3 slices of veal. Garnish with remaining chervil and lemon zest. Serve immediately.

*The bounty of the Midwest's streams and fields makes possible the pleasures of Grilled Brook Trout
and Vegetable Kabobs with Lime-Dill Sauce.*

GRILLED BROOK TROUT AND VEGETABLE KABOBS WITH LIME-DILL SAUCE

Recommended Wine: Sauvignon Blanc

6 SERVINGS

6 fresh whole brook trout (6 to 8 ounces
each), cleaned
8 tablespoons unsalted butter, melted
¼ teaspoon salt
⅛ teaspoon freshly ground pepper
12 cherry tomatoes
12 medium-large mushroom caps
2 small zucchini, cut into 1-inch chunks
1 red onion, cut into 6 wedges
1 yellow or green bell pepper, seeded and
cut into 1-inch chunks
Lime-Dill Sauce (recipe follows)

Rinse fish inside and out with cold running water. Pat dry with paper towels. Brush cavities of trout with 4 tablespoons butter and sprinkle with salt and pepper.

Thread vegetables in an alternating pattern onto twelve 6-inch metal or bamboo skewers.

Prepare charcoal, gas or electric grill.

Grill fish and vegetable kabobs 4 to 6 inches from heat until lightly browned, 3 minutes for fish, 1 to 2 minutes for vegetables. Brush fish and vegetables with remaining 4 tablespoons melted butter and turn. Cook until fish flakes easily with a fork and vegetables are crisp-tender, 2 to 3 minutes longer for fish, and 1 to 2 minutes longer for vegetables.

To serve, place one grilled trout and 2 vegetable skewers on each plate. Pass Lime-Dill Sauce separately.

LIME-DILL SAUCE

MAKES 1½ CUPS

3 eggs, lightly beaten
1½ cups plain yogurt
2 to 3 tablespoons minced fresh dill or 2
to 3 teaspoons dried dill
1 teaspoon grated lime zest
½ teaspoon salt
Dash of cayenne pepper

In small nonreactive saucepan, beat eggs and yogurt until well blended. Cook over medium low heat, stirring constantly, until mixture thickens and coats spoon, about 10 minutes.

Stir in dill, lime zest, salt and cayenne.

Serve hot.

PEPPERED STEAK WELLINGTON

Recommended Wine: Zinfandel

6 SERVINGS

¼   cup olive oil
1   teaspoon coarsely ground pepper
½   teaspoon crushed red pepper flakes
6   beef tenderloins, cut 1-inch thick (each
     about 4 ounces)
     Salt to taste
2   medium-size green bell peppers, seeded
     and finely diced
1   large red bell pepper, seeded and finely
     diced
3   sheets (10 × 10-inches each) frozen
     prepared puff pastry

In large skillet, warm 2 tablespoons oil over medium-high heat. Add black pepper and red pepper flakes and sauté until hot.

Add beef and quickly brown for 3 to 4 minutes on each side. Transfer beef to platter. Salt to taste.

Cover and refrigerate until just chilled, about 30 minutes.

In medium skillet over medium-high heat, sauté bell peppers in remaining 2 tablespoons oil. Cook, stirring frequently, until peppers are tender and browned, 10 to 15 minutes.

Transfer to a plate. Cover and refrigerate until just chilled, about 30 minutes.

Preheat oven to 425 degrees.

Arrange frozen puff pastry sheets in a single layer on lightly floured surface; thaw 5 minutes. With sharp knife, cut each puff pastry sheet in half to form six 10 × 5-inch rectangles.

Place 1 tenderloin in center of each puff pastry rectangle. Divide cooked, cooled peppers evenly over top of beef.

Lightly brush edges of pastry with water. Fold puff pastry over peppers and beef, overlapping edges and press gently to seal pastry sheets; smooth out seams.

Place Wellingtons on lightly greased baking sheets. Bake until pastry is golden, 20 to 25 minutes.

Serve hot.

BOURBON-GLAZED ROAST PHEASANT

Recommended Wine: Cabernet Sauvignon

6 SERVINGS

2   *medium celery roots (celeriac) (1 to 1½ pounds total weight)*
3   *whole pheasants (each about 2¼ to 2½ pounds, dressed)*
3   *tablespoons vegetable oil*
8   *tablespoons unsalted butter*
3   *cups chopped fresh cranberries*
2   *leeks, cleaned and sliced, including some green*
1   *cup dark raisins*
½   *teaspoon salt*
¼   *teaspoon freshly ground pepper*
½   *cup packed dark brown sugar*
⅓   *cup bourbon*
¼   *cup dark molasses*

Peel celery roots and cut into ½-inch chunks. In steamer basket over boiling water, cook celery roots until tender, about 10 minutes.

Rinse pheasants inside and out and pat dry with paper towels.

In large skillet, heat oil over medium high heat. Add pheasants, one at a time, and cook, turning often, until lightly browned all over, about 5 minutes. Remove from heat and set aside to cool for 10 minutes. Reserve skillet.

Preheat oven to 325 degrees.

Add 4 tablespoons butter, celery root, cranberries, leeks, raisins, salt and pepper to drippings in skillet. Sauté, stirring frequently, until leeks are soft, about 5 minutes. Remove from heat and set aside to cool for 10 minutes.

Lightly stuff pheasants with cranberry mixture; fold skin over opening. Place pheasants, breast side up, on a rack in a shallow roasting pan.

In small skillet, melt remaining 4 tablespoons butter. Stir in brown sugar, bourbon and molasses until well blended.

Brush pheasants with bourbon glaze. Cover loosely with foil. Roast for 30 minutes.

Remove foil, brush with bourbon glaze. Roast, uncovered, basting twice more with bourbon glaze, until juices run clear when thigh is pierced with a fork and the legs move easily when lifted and turned, about 30 minutes longer.

To serve, slice and arrange meat on heated serving platter. Spoon dressing onto serving plates.

OVERLEAF: Only honest, basic ingredients are required to make Hot Buttered Rum Apple Pie, the perfect way to finish off a hearty Midwestern dinner.

HAZELNUT FUDGE MOUSSE

8 SERVINGS

6   ounces bittersweet chocolate
2   ounces unsweetened chocolate
¼   cup hazelnut liqueur, such as Frangelico
5   eggs, separated
½   teaspoon cream of tartar
1   cup heavy cream
½   cup finely chopped toasted hazelnuts

In double boiler over hot, not boiling, water, melt bittersweet and unsweetened chocolate with liqueur, stirring occasionally. Remove from heat.

With wire whisk, beat egg yolks into chocolate mixture until smooth; set aside to cool to room temperature.

In large mixing bowl, beat egg whites and cream of tartar with electric mixer at high speed until stiff peaks form. Fold into chocolate mixture.

In large mixing bowl, beat cream at high speed until stiff peaks form. Fold into chocolate mixture.

Spoon mousse into 8 individual 8- or 10-ounce glass dishes or ramekins and refrigerate until set, about 3 hours.

To serve, garnish with chopped hazelnuts.

HOT BUTTERED RUM APPLE PIE

Recommended Wine: Late Harvest White Riesling

6 TO 8 SERVINGS

     Butter Pie Pastry (recipe follows)
8   tablespoons unsalted butter
½   cup firmly packed light brown sugar
1   tablespoon fresh lemon juice
1   teaspoon grated lemon zest
¼   teaspoon freshly grated nutmeg
8   tart green apples, such as Granny
        Smith, pared, cored and sliced
1   tablespoon cornstarch
¼   cup light rum
½   cup granulated sugar
½   cup all-purpose flour
¼   cup sliced almonds

Prepare Butter Pie Pastry; set aside.

Preheat oven to 375 degrees.

In large skillet over medium low heat, melt 4 tablespoons butter. Stir in brown sugar, lemon juice, lemon zest, nutmeg and apples. Reduce heat to low, cover and simmer, stirring occasionally, until apples are tender, about 10 minutes.

In small bowl, blend cornstarch and rum until smooth. Stir into apple mixture and cook, stirring constantly, until thickened, about 1 minute. Remove from heat and set aside.

On lightly floured surface, roll out dough ⅛ inch thick. Fit pastry gently into 9-inch pie plate. Trim and flute edge.

Pour apple mixture into unbaked pie shell.

In small bowl, blend remaining 4 tablespoons butter, granulated sugar and flour with pastry blender or 2 knives until mixture resembles coarse crumbs; stir in almonds.

Sprinkle flour mixture over apples.

Bake pie until golden brown, 30 to 35 minutes. Remove from oven and cool on wire rack for 15 minutes before cutting into wedges to serve.

BUTTER PIE PASTRY

MAKES ONE 9-INCH SINGLE CRUST PIE SHELL

1⅓   *cups all-purpose flour*
¼   *teaspoon salt*
8   *tablespoons cold unsalted butter, cut into bits*
1   *egg yolk*
2   *tablespoons ice water*

Stir flour and salt together in medium bowl. Cut in butter with pastry blender or 2 knives until mixture resembles coarse crumbs.

In small bowl, blend together egg yolk and ice water with fork. Sprinkle over flour mixture and mix lightly with fork just until dough begins to stick together. Add more water as needed to form dough.

Press dough into ball; wrap in plastic wrap and refrigerate for at least 30 minutes.

THE SOUTH

RECIPES

Okra Ratatouille Soup with Sun-Dried Tomatoes

Shrimp Canapés

Chive Butter Croutons

Flaky Buttermilk Biscuits

*Fresh Vegetable Julienne
and Chilled Rice Salad*

Soraparo

Creamy Herbed Sweet Potatoes

Turnip Greens and Potlikker

Black-Eyed Peas

Fried Chicken

*Gulf States Red Snapper Broiled
with Blue Cheese*

Pompano in Parchment

Sirloin Steak Diane

Marinated Grilled Swordfish

*Florida Pork Chops with
Black Bean Purée and Fresh Fruit*

Baba Au Rhum

Key West Lime Pie

Peach Pie

Everglade Bananas

Defining the heart and soul of Dixie requires more than a map and a history text. The American South is a past and a presence, a sensuous, stubborn, living, breathing spirit. If you are to taste it, touch it, smell it, or ever truly know it, you must explore its food. For, in fact, the heart and soul of the South are found in its stomach.

If a single word embodies the essential Southern experience, that word is "barbecue." That's right—"barbecue." And why not? The word's Caribbean origins link it to the region's earliest immigrants; it comes from the Haitian-Spanish *barbacoe*, referring at first to a wooden rack on which meats were grilled and, later, to the grilling itself. The strong, hearty flavors of barbecue place it smack in the mainstream of down-home plantation cooking, a style dedicated to the expansive appreciation of the well-stocked larder. And its position center stage at virtually any public celebration, political rally, or charitable fundraiser constitutes Southern hospitality at its best.

To a Southerner, barbecue means but one thing: whole, pit-roasted pig, slow cooked for twelve or sixteen hours over hickory coals. Beyond that, arguments abound. In North Carolina the tender, smoky meat is cooled, chopped, smothered in sauces, reheated, and heaped on great gloppy buns. In Georgia, where politickin' and pig-pickin' are inseparable, the cooked pig is carved immediately and the meat eaten right off the bone. In some places folks enjoy their barbecue sliced, while elsewhere such a proposal is greeted with jeers. As expected, there are as many different barbecue sauces as there are pigs, but all the best sauces are spicy hot, smoky sweet, and generously ladled on.

There's less argument about side dishes to accompany barbecue. For starters, you must have grits. Grits are kernels of dried corn, ground and boiled. Simple, filling and infinitely versatile, they are a Southern institution. After grits come pickles, from homemade dills to watermelon rind and pickled peaches. Then there are pepper relishes, corn breads, sweet potato casseroles, and salads and greens of endless invention. And last but not least, coleslaw, hush puppies and Brunswick stew—all barbecue basics, all served hog by jowl with the entrée at roadhouses throughout the South.

Every Southern cook has an original wrinkle that redefines these classics. Some like their Brunswick with okra, some with just onions; pragmatists preach chicken, while purists demand squirrel. Even hush puppies—which are nothing more than deep-fried cornmeal dumplings—are tinkered with, some cooks adding beer to the batter, some chopping onions or peppers into the meal, and some omitting egg yolks and buttermilk to lighten them up.

PRECEDING OVERLEAF: The Florida Everglades, one of America's great wildlife preserves, is a place of awe-inspiring beauty and serenity.

ABOVE: A stunning sunset at Key West, Florida.

Today, as always, fried foods constitute the basis of much Southern cooking. Southerners will seemingly fry anything, including yams, peas, and dill pickles, but fish and chicken are the most enduringly popular. Nothing gets a Southern chef going like a good debate over the nuances of cutting, seasoning, battering, cooking and even draining fried chicken. No matter how many authentic Southern fried chicken recipes you consult, there will be only two points of consistency: none will resemble any other in its particulars; and all will insist that its the only one to use.

Tradition notwithstanding, the winds of cholesterol-consciousness are blowing across the South and adding new choices to the old favorites. Seafood restaurants now encourage customers to select not only their fish, but also its method of preparation. True, there's still catfish, and yes it's still fried if you insist, but it can also be broiled, grilled, or blackened. The simplest preparation is often the best: lightly grilled and sprinkled with the juice of ripe Key limes.

The South, no less than any coastal area, is fish-rich.

LEFT: An Everglades fisherman makes a catch.
The South is a region of vast agricultural wealth: (above) a rice field; (opposite, top) pigs at leisure; (center) a beekeeper at work; (bottom) fishing in Georgia.

It is awash in redfish, grouper, flounder, snapper, mackerel, and the delicate, much-admired pompano. Florida in particular enjoys a variety of even more exotic aquatic fare, from frog's legs to conch chowder, turtle steaks to 'gator tails (texture of lobster, taste of chicken and fish). Just as impressive are Florida's shellfish. The stone crabs from the brackish waters of the Everglades have shells so hard they must be cracked with a mallet, and flesh so tender it melts butter. Crayfish and scallops abound, oysters are roasted by the bushel, and fat, sweet shrimp—boiled, broiled, and plopped into pies, patties, and pilau (or "purloo")—have been consumed with unremitting gusto for centuries.

This unique bounty is equaled by the produce of the land. To the usual vegetables—corn, potatoes, tomatoes, rice, and beans—are added okra, yams, peppers, black-eyed peas, and greens of every description. Immense, flavorful berries flourish, along with melons, peaches, cherries, oranges, grapefruit, lemons, and limes. And tropical delicacies like avocados, mangoes, guavas, and *platanos*—green bananas that are sliced thin and fried like potato chips—thrive.

The foods and spices of the tropics have always held sway around Key West, and Spanish settlers first brought beans, peanuts, rum, cayenne, Tabasco, and exotic spices from there to the mainland more than four centuries ago. Today the scents of Caribbean-inspired soups and sausages fill the streets of cities from Miami to Tampa. *Bollos*—black-eyed peas, garlic, and onions ground into a paste, seasoned with dried hot pepper, shaped into balls, and deep-fried—and black sausage and black bean soup, are as entrenched in the southern half of the state as pompano *en papillote* is in the north.

Waves of immigrants have left their mark on Florida's cooking. Seminoles, Spaniards, Cubans, Conchs, Italians, Greeks, Moroccans—the influences are too diverse to untangle completely. The same holds true throughout much of the South. An English sea captain, John Thurber, brought a bag of long-grain Madagascar rice to Charleston in 1680, giving birth to an industry that has prospered there for three centuries. At the same time an unknown black man, newly arrived on a slave ship, transplanted the first benne (sesame) seeds he had smuggled from Africa. They quickly became a low-cost, high-protein staple, used in stews, breads, "good luck" cookies, and crisp candy.

At home, black cooks would prepare such simple, hearty fare as "Hoppin' John"—black-eyed peas and rice; but in the white man's kitchen they applied their hot-climate spicing skills to classic French recipes imported by the Huguenots, who had come fleeing religious persecution in France. A distinctive French style of Southern cooking resulted, making Charleston famous and adding still another influence to the region's overflowing board.

In many respects, the rich gravies, boiled vegetables, and fried fish and meats that occupy the traditional Southern table seem out of step with current fashion. But other regional mainstays are more popular than ever. Our infatuation with grilling is an extension of our longstanding love affair with barbecue. Our interest in hot peppers and spices reflects our Caribbean, as well as Central American, heritage. And our present-day passion for sweets, the richer the better, was never anywhere more catered to than in the South.

There, at even the simplest barbecue, the hungry visitor will find jellies and jams, relishes and chutneys,

The well-stocked Southern pantry invariably contains a shelf of homemade jams and preserves, sometimes using locally grown lemons and other fruits.

meringues, puddings, pies, pralines, cakes, tarts, trifles, and turnovers—in short, the whole universe of decadence—displayed in heartbreaking profusion. There, in time-honored Southern fashion, the host will heap up the guest's plate, steer him toward a shady chair, and enjoin him to settle back for some serious eating.

That's Southern hospitality. That's the magic of the South.

From marinas such as this one in the Florida Keys, fishermen set out to catch red snapper, pompano, and other local delicacies.

OKRA RATATOUILLE SOUP WITH SUN-DRIED TOMATOES

Recommended Wine: Rosé of Cabernet

6 SERVINGS

2   medium onions, chopped
3   tablespoons olive oil
1   pound baby okra, ends trimmed
1   bunch fresh basil, trimmed
1½ ounces sun-dried tomatoes (about 16
       halves)
1   quart rich homemade chicken broth
1   cup dry white wine
1   teaspoon salt
¼   teaspoon freshly ground pepper

In medium saucepan, sauté onions in oil over medium-high heat until soft, about 5 minutes.

Add okra, basil and tomatoes and cook until okra is crisp-tender, 5 to 7 minutes.

Stir in broth, wine, salt and pepper. Simmer, covered, until heated through, about 15 minutes.

To serve, ladle hot soup into a tureen or serve in individual bowls.

SHRIMP CANAPES

Recommended Wine: Johannisberg Riesling

MAKES 48 CANAPES

½   teaspoon salt
1   pound raw medium shrimp
2   medium ribs celery, finely chopped
¼   cup mayonnaise
2   teaspoons fresh lemon juice
2   teaspoons chopped fresh chives
¼   teaspoon salt
⅛   teaspoon freshly ground white pepper
       Chive Butter Croutons (recipe follows)
       Paprika

In a medium saucepan, bring about 2 cups water and salt to a boil over high heat. Add shrimp; cook until shrimp become firm and turn pink, 2 to 3 minutes. Rinse shrimp under cold running water; drain. Remove shells; devein, if desired.

Finely chop shrimp or process 5 seconds in a food processor fitted with a metal blade.

In small bowl, combine shrimp, celery, mayonnaise, lemon juice, chives, salt and pepper.

To serve, top each Chive Butter Crouton with about 2 teaspoons shrimp mixture.

Serve immediately or cover with plastic wrap and refrigerate until chilled, about 1 hour. Garnish each canapé with paprika.

PRECEDING OVERLEAF: Okra is one of the South's most distinctive vegetables; this Okra Ratatouille Soup with Sun-Dried Tomatoes is an innovative way to serve it.

CHIVE BUTTER CROUTONS

MAKES 48 CROUTONS

12 very thin slices firm-textured white
      bread
2   tablespoons melted unsalted butter
2   teaspoons finely chopped fresh chives

Preheat oven to 300 degrees.

Trim crusts from bread and cut each slice diagonally into 4 triangles.

Arrange triangles in a single layer on a baking sheet. Bake, turning once, until dry and lightly toasted, 10 to 15 minutes.

Meanwhile, combine butter and chives. Brush warm croutons with butter mixture.

FLAKY BUTTERMILK BISCUITS

MAKES 15 BISCUITS

1   package active dry yeast
3   tablespoons sugar
1   cup buttermilk
½   teaspoon salt
2½   cups self-rising flour
½   cup shortening

In small bowl, combine 3 tablespoons lukewarm water (110° to 115°F), yeast and 1 teaspoon sugar. Let stand until bubbly, about 5 minutes.

Meanwhile, heat buttermilk and salt in small saucepan over low heat until just warm, not hot. Add to yeast mixture.

In medium bowl, combine flour and remaining 2 tablespoons plus 2 teaspoons sugar. Cut in shortening with pastry blender or 2 knives until mixture resembles coarse crumbs. Add yeast mixture to flour mixture; knead just until dough sticks together.

On lightly floured surface, roll out dough ½ inch thick.

Using floured 3-inch biscuit cutter or rim of glass, cut out 15 circles of dough, rerolling scraps of dough, if necessary. Place on lightly greased baking sheet.

Cover and let rise in warm place (80 to 85 degrees) until doubled in bulk, about 1 hour.

Preheat oven to 400 degrees.

Bake biscuits until golden brown, 10 to 12 minutes. Serve hot.

OVERLEAF: *Fresh Vegetable Julienne and Chilled Rice Salad is a Southern tradition and is often served at picnics and barbecues on warm summer days.*

FRESH VEGETABLE JULIENNE AND CHILLED RICE SALAD

Recommended Wine: Chenin Blanc

6 TO 8 SERVINGS

½   *teaspoon salt*
1   *teaspoon vegetable oil*
1   *cup long-grain white rice*
1   *cup shelled fresh peas*
⅓   *cup mayonnaise*
¼   *cup tarragon white wine vinegar*
1   *small green bell pepper, seeded and cut*
       into 1-inch-long julienne
1   *small red bell pepper, seeded and cut*
       into 1-inch-long julienne
1   *small cucumber, peeled, seeded and*
       diced
½   *teaspoon salt*
½   *teaspoon dried tarragon, crushed*
⅛   *teaspoon freshly ground pepper*
2   *to 3 Belgian endive, trimmed and*
       separated

In medium saucepan, combine salt and oil with 2¼ cups water. Bring to a boil over high heat.

Stir in rice, and reduce heat to low.

Cover and simmer until rice is cooked and has absorbed all liquid, 20 to 25 minutes.

Remove from heat and spoon into bowl. Cover and refrigerate until chilled, 1 to 2 hours.

In a small saucepan, blanch peas in boiling water to cover for 3 to 4 minutes, until barely tender. Rinse under cold running water; drain.

In large bowl, combine chilled rice, peas, mayonnaise, vinegar, green and red bell peppers, cucumber, salt, tarragon and pepper. Cover and refrigerate until chilled, 4 hours or overnight, to allow flavors to blend.

To serve, arrange 3 to 4 endive leaves on each salad plate. Spoon rice mixture evenly on top of endive. Serve immediately.

SORAPARO

6 TO 8 SERVINGS

1   *tablespoon unsalted butter*
2   *tablespoons peanut oil*
1   *large red onion, peeled and sliced*
1   *large white sweet onion, such as*
       Vidalia, peeled and sliced
1   *large yellow onion, peeled and sliced*
2   *leeks, washed well and sliced*
2   *teaspoons Worcestershire sauce*
1   *teaspoon dry mustard*
1   *teaspoon salt*
⅛   *teaspoon freshly ground pepper*
3   *green onions, including green tops,*
       chopped

Heat butter and oil in large skillet over medium high heat. Add all of the onions and leeks and stir in Worcestershire sauce, dry mustard, salt and pepper. Sauté, stirring occasionally, until onions and leeks are golden brown and tender, about 15 minutes.

Serve, garnished with green onions.

CREAMY HERBED SWEET POTATOES

6 SERVINGS

2   to 2½ pounds sweet potatoes or yams
4   ounces double-crème cheese with herbs
2   eggs
1   tablespoon chopped fresh tarragon
2   tablespoons chopped fresh parsley
¼   teaspoon salt
⅛   teaspoon freshly ground white pepper

In large saucepan, bring 3 quarts water to a boil over high heat. Add potatoes and boil until tender when pierced with a fork, about 20 minutes. Drain and peel potatoes.

Preheat oven to 425 degrees. Lightly butter six 1-cup ramekins.

In a bowl, combine potatoes with cheese, eggs, tarragon, parsley, salt and pepper. Beat with electric mixer at high speed until smooth.

Spoon potato mixture into pastry bag fitted with ½-inch star tip. Divide potato mixture among the prepared baking dishes.

Bake until lightly browned, about 15 minutes. Serve hot.

TURNIP GREENS AND POTLIKKER

6 SERVINGS

½   pound salt pork, cut into 1-inch cubes
2   pounds turnip greens, washed and
        trimmed
¼   teaspoon freshly ground pepper

In 5-quart Dutch oven, bring 3 quarts water and salt pork to a boil over high heat. Reduce heat to low, cover and simmer for 30 minutes.

Stir in turnip greens and bring to a boil over high heat.

Reduce heat to low and simmer until greens are tender, about 30 minutes.

Drain; discard salt pork. Arrange greens on heated serving platter and sprinkle with pepper. Serve hot.

BLACK-EYED PEAS

6 SERVINGS

2   cups shelled fresh black-eyed peas
¼   teaspoon salt
      Hot pepper sauce

In large saucepan, bring peas, salt and 6 cups water to a boil over high heat.

Reduce heat to low, cover and simmer until peas are tender, 15 to 20 minutes. Drain.

Serve hot, sprinkled with hot pepper sauce.

Creamy Herbed Sweet Potatoes—a hearty dish with the subtle flavor of fresh tarragon and parsley.

FRIED CHICKEN

Recommended Wine: Fumé Blanc
6 TO 8 SERVINGS

2   broiler/fryer chickens (about 7 pounds total weight), cut into serving pieces
2   cups buttermilk
2   cups half-and-half
2   cups self-rising flour
1   teaspoon salt
1   teaspoon paprika
½   teaspoon freshly ground pepper
    Vegetable oil for frying
    Creamy Gravy (recipe follows)
    Dried rosemary

Wash chicken and pat dry with paper towels.

Pour buttermilk and half-and-half into large bowl. Add chicken pieces and turn to coat completely. Cover and refrigerate for about 1 hour, turning chicken occasionally.

Drain chicken, reserving buttermilk marinade. In large shallow dish, combine flour, salt, paprika and pepper. One at a time, dredge chicken pieces in flour mixture, shaking off excess. Place coated chicken on a wire rack. Repeat until all of chicken is coated.

Let chicken stand for 30 minutes at room temperature.

In large heavy skillet, heat ½ inch vegetable oil to 375 degrees. A few pieces at a time, add chicken, skin side down, and fry, turning often, until richly browned, crisp and cooked through, about 20 minutes. Drain on paper towels. Reserve drippings.

Serve immediately with Creamy Gravy and garnish with rosemary.

CREAMY GRAVY

MAKES 4 CUPS GRAVY

¼   cup reserved fried chicken drippings
⅓   cup all-purpose flour
1½   teaspoons salt
½   teaspoon freshly ground pepper
    Reserved buttermilk marinade (about 3 cups)
1   cup milk

After frying chicken, return ¼ cup drippings to skillet. Stir in flour, salt and pepper and cook over medium heat until bubbly. Reduce heat to low.

Gradually blend in buttermilk mixture and milk and continue cooking and stirring until gravy bubbles and thickens.

Remove from heat and serve with chicken.

Fried Chicken—the crowning glory of Southern home cooking.

GULF STATES RED SNAPPER BROILED WITH BLUE CHEESE

Recommended Wine: Chardonnay

6 TO 8 SERVINGS

2 to 6 tablespoons unsalted butter
2 to 6 tablespoons olive oil
2 large onions, peeled and sliced
3 to 4 small red chile peppers, plus
    additional chiles for garnish, if
    desired
2 bay leaves
2 pounds red snapper fillets
1/4 teaspoon salt
1/8 teaspoon freshly ground pepper
1/4 teaspoon dried oregano, crumbled
    Juice of 1/2 lemon
2 tablespoons (1 ounce) crumbled blue
    cheese
2 tablespoons chopped fresh parsley
    Lemon wedges

Preheat oven to 225 degrees. Place an ovenproof platter in oven to warm.

In large skillet, melt 2 tablespoons butter with 2 tablespoons oil over medium heat. Add onions, chiles and bay leaves and cook, stirring frequently, until onions are golden, about 20 minutes.

Transfer to heated platter and keep warm in oven while cooking snapper.

Rinse fish fillets under cold running water and pat dry with paper towels. Lightly grease a 13 × 9 × 2-inch baking dish.

In a large skillet, melt 2 tablespoons butter with 2 tablespoons oil over medium heat. Add as many fillets as fit in a single layer and season lightly with salt, pepper and oregano. Cook until lightly browned and fish flakes easily with a fork, 3 to 4 minutes on each side.

Layer fillets in the prepared baking dish, cover and keep warm.

Repeat sautéing and layering with remaining butter, oil and fillets.

Remove platter from oven and preheat broiler.

Spoon warm onion mixture over fish and sprinkle with lemon juice and blue cheese.

Broil 4 to 5 inches from heat until cheese melts, 3 to 5 minutes. Remove bay leaves. Garnish with parsley and additional red chile peppers, if desired, and serve with lemon wedges.

The waters of the Gulf Coast teem with fish, making Alabama, Mississippi, and Florida famous for dishes such as Gulf States Red Snapper Broiled with Blue Cheese.

Pompano in Parchment—an elegant preparation for special guests.

POMPANO IN PARCHMENT

Recommended Wine: Semillon

8 SERVINGS

¼   cup minced shallots
3   tablespoons olive oil
2   medium carrots, pared
3   leeks, white part only, trimmed and
        washed well
8   pompano fillets (6 ounces each)
2   ounces fresh oyster mushrooms, wiped,
        trimmed and broken into large bite-
        sized pieces
    Salt
    Freshly ground pepper
    Grand Marnier Glaze (recipe follows)

Cut 8 heart-shaped pieces of parchment paper, large enough to enclose fish.

Preheat oven to 450 degrees.

In medium skillet, sauté shallots in oil over medium heat for 3 minutes; remove from heat.

Cut carrots and leeks in 4-inch-long julienne. Add to shallots and toss until combined.

Dividing equally, spoon vegetables onto one side of each parchment heart. Top each portion with 1 fish fillet and some oyster mushrooms. Sprinkle with salt and pepper. Fold over parchment and crimp and twist edges to close.

Arrange parchment packets on 2 baking sheets and bake until puffed and browned, 7 to 10 minutes.

Serve on dinner plates and slit open packages in front of each person. Pass the Grand Marnier Glaze separately.

GRAND MARNIER GLAZE

MAKES 1 CUP

¼   cup minced leeks, white part only
¼   cup chopped carrots
¼   cup minced shallots
3   tablespoons unsalted butter
¼   cup raspberry vinegar
    Juice of 5 oranges (about 1½ cups) plus
        1 orange, thinly sliced
3   tablespoons Grand Marnier
2   teaspoons all-purpose flour

In small saucepan, sauté leeks, carrots and shallots in 2 tablespoons butter over medium heat until soft, 5 to 7 minutes.

Stir in vinegar, orange juice and sliced orange; bring to a boil over medium high heat. Cook until reduced by half, about 10 minutes.

Stir in Grand Marnier.

Combine remaining 1 tablespoon butter with the flour and whisk in, ½ teaspoon at a time, until mixture thickens.

Strain through a fine sieve and serve immediately with baked pompano.

SIRLOIN STEAK DIANE

Recommended Wine: Cabernet Sauvignon
6 SERVINGS

3   *pounds sirloin, cut into six 1-inch thick steaks*
6   *cloves garlic, crushed*
2   *tablespoons dried parsley*
1   *tablespoon dried rosemary, crumbled*
1   *teaspoon ground sage*
4   *bay leaves, crumbled*
     Freshly ground pepper
3   *tablespoons olive oil*
3   *tablespoons Cognac, warmed*

Rub steaks with garlic. Sprinkle both sides of steaks with parsley, rosemary, sage, bay leaves and black pepper.

In heavy 12-inch skillet over high heat, heat oil. Add steaks and sauté for 3 to 4 minutes. Turn and sauté 3 minutes for rare, 5 minutes for medium-rare.

Pour Cognac over steaks and carefully ignite. Sauté, shaking pan until flames subside.

Serve immediately.

MARINATED GRILLED SWORDFISH

Recommended Wine: Chardonnay or Merlot
6 SERVINGS

3   *pounds swordfish, cut into six 1-inch thick steaks*
1   *cup medium-dry sherry*
4   *green onions, including some of the greens, chopped*
6   *to 8 sprigs fresh tarragon*
1/3 *cup olive oil*

Arrange swordfish in a single layer in 13 × 9-inch non-metal baking dish or in large re-closable plastic bag. Add sherry, onions and tarragon. Cover dish or close bag and refrigerate for 1½ to 2 hours, turning once.

Prepare charcoal, gas or electric grill. Place grill 4 to 6 inches above heat.

Drain swordfish and tarragon; discard marinade.

Brush swordfish with some oil. Arrange tarragon under swordfish and grill until lightly browned, 5 to 6 minutes.

Turn and brush swordfish with more oil, arranging tarragon under fish. Continue grilling until swordfish flakes with a fork, about 5 minutes.

Serve hot.

FLORIDA PORK CHOPS WITH BLACK BEAN PUREE AND FRESH FRUIT

Recommended Wine: Zinfandel

6 SERVINGS

½   cup dried black beans, washed and
        picked over
2   cups rich homemade chicken stock
2   cloves garlic, minced
¼   cup chopped onion
3   tablespoons olive oil
2   tablespoons fresh lime juice
2   tablespoons white wine vinegar
2   tablespoons chopped fresh oregano
¼   cup chopped cilantro
     Dash of cayenne pepper
     Salt
6   pork loin rib chops, each cut 1½-inches
        thick
1   papaya or 2 mangoes, peeled, seeded
        and sliced
2   kiwi fruits, peeled and sliced

In small saucepan, bring beans and stock to a boil over high heat.

Reduce heat to low, cover and simmer until beans are tender, 1½ to 2 hours.

Purée cooked beans in blender or food processor; set aside.

In small skillet, sauté garlic and onion in 1 tablespoon olive oil over medium high heat.

Add puréed beans, lime juice, vinegar, oregano, cilantro, cayenne and 1 cup water. Cook, stirring frequently, until mixture is thickened and bubbly, about 10 minutes. Season to taste with salt. Keep warm over low heat.

Preheat oven to 325 degrees. Lightly oil a 3-quart baking dish.

In large skillet over high heat, brown pork chops in remaining 2 tablespoons olive oil for 4 to 6 minutes on each side.

Transfer to prepared baking dish. Cover and bake until tender, about 1½ hours.

To serve, spoon hot black bean purée over baked pork chops. Garnish with fresh fruit.

BABA AU RHUM

Recommended Wine: White Riesling

10 TO 12 SERVINGS

1½   cups all-purpose flour
1½   teaspoons baking powder
¼   teaspoon salt
½   cup milk
4   tablespoons unsalted butter
5   eggs
1   cup sugar
1   teaspoon vanilla extract

1   teaspoon rum extract
     Hot Rum Sauce (recipe follows)
1   cup heavy cream
2   tablespoons powdered sugar
1   tablespoon rum
1   kiwi fruit, peeled and sliced
1   cup fresh strawberries, hulled and
        halved

Baba au Rhum—a Southern variation on a classic European dessert.

Preheat oven to 350 degrees. Grease and flour a 10-inch tube pan.

On a sheet of waxed paper, sift together flour, baking powder and salt; set aside.

In small saucepan, combine milk and butter over medium low heat until butter melts (do not allow milk to boil).

In large mixing bowl, beat eggs with electric mixer at high speed until very thick and lemon colored, about 7 minutes.

Gradually beat in sugar, vanilla and rum extract; beat 3 to 4 minutes longer. Add flour mixture and beat just until smooth. Beat in milk mixture just until blended.

Turn batter into prepared cake pan. Bake until cake springs back when touched lightly with finger, 25 to 30 minutes.

Cool cake in pan on wire rack for 15 minutes. Unmold.

Reserving ¼ cup, pour remaining Hot Rum Sauce on large serving plate with rim. Place cake, top side down, onto sauce. Drizzle reserved sauce over cake.

Cover loosely with plastic wrap; let cool to room temperature.

When ready to serve, whip cream in medium bowl until soft peaks form. Add powdered sugar and rum and continue beating until stiff peaks form.

Spoon whipped cream into pastry bag fitted with a fluted pastry tip. Pipe cream decoratively in middle of cake, filling up center and forming a pyramid. Pipe about 8 rosettes of whipped cream around bottom edge of cake.

Just before serving, arrange sliced kiwi and strawberries on whipped cream, overlapping slightly.

HOT RUM SAUCE

MAKES ABOUT 1 CUP

½ *cup honey*
½ *cup firmly packed dark brown sugar*
3 *tablespoons unsalted butter*
3 *tablespoons rum*

In medium saucepan, bring honey, sugar, butter and 2 tablespoons water to a boil over high heat. Cook, stirring constantly, until sugar dissolves, 3 to 5 minutes. Remove from heat and stir in rum.

KEY WEST LIME PIE

6 SERVINGS

1¼   cups graham cracker crumbs
½   cup plus 2 tablespoons sugar
¼   cup unsalted butter, melted
¼   teaspoon ground cinnamon
    Dash of freshly grated nutmeg
6   eggs, separated
2   cans (14 ounces each) sweetened
      condensed milk
1¼   cups key lime juice or regular lime juice
½   teaspoon cream of tartar

In small bowl, blend graham cracker crumbs, 2 tablespoons sugar, butter, cinnamon and nutmeg until evenly moistened. Press crumb mixture into bottom and up sides of 9-inch pie plate; set aside.

Preheat oven to 375 degrees.

In medium bowl, combine egg yolks, condensed milk and lime juice; blend until smooth. Pour mixture into crumb crust-lined pie plate; set aside.

In large mixing bowl with electric mixer at high speed, beat egg whites and cream of tartar until foamy. Gradually beat in remaining ½ cup sugar, 1 tablespoon at a time, until sugar is dissolved and whites form glossy stiff peaks.

Spread meringue over filling reaching all the way to edges, swirling to form peaks.

Bake until peaks are lightly browned, 5 to 7 minutes. Cool to room temperature.

Refrigerate for 8 hours or overnight before cutting into wedges to serve.

PEACH PIE

6 SERVINGS

    Pie Pastry (recipe follows)
6   cups peeled sliced peaches
⅓   cup packed light brown sugar
¼   cup plus 2 tablespoons all-purpose flour
1   tablespoon cornstarch
¾   teaspoon ground cinnamon
¼   teaspoon ground cardamom
    Dash of freshly grated nutmeg
2   tablespoons fresh lemon juice
1⅓   cups granola
¼   cup sliced almonds
¼   cup unsalted butter, melted
2   tablespoons honey

Prepare Pie Pastry; prebake and set aside.

Reduce oven temperature to 375 degrees.

In large bowl, combine peaches, brown sugar, 2 tablespoons flour, cornstarch, ½ teaspoon cinnamon, cardamom, nutmeg and lemon juice. Turn into prebaked pie crust.

In medium bowl, combine remaining ¼ cup flour, remaining ¼ teaspoon cinnamon, granola, almonds, butter and honey until ingredients are well blended. Sprinkle over peaches.

Bake until richly browned, 30 to 35 minutes. Cool on wire rack.

Serve warm or refrigerate until chilled, about 6 hours.

PIE PASTRY

MAKES ONE 9-INCH SINGLE CRUST PIE SHELL

1⅓ cups all-purpose flour
¼ teaspoon salt
⅓ cup solid vegetable shortening, chilled
4 to 6 tablespoons ice water

Stir flour and salt together in medium bowl. Cut in shortening with pastry blender or 2 knives until mixture resembles coarse crumbs.

Sprinkle 4 tablespoons ice water over flour mixture, mixing lightly with fork just until dough sticks together. Add more water, 1 tablespoon at a time, as needed to form dough.

Press into ball, cover and refrigerate, 30 minutes.

Preheat oven to 450 degrees.

On lightly floured surface, roll out dough ⅛ inch thick.

Fit pastry gently into 9-inch pie plate. Trim and flute edge. Prick bottom and sides of crust with fork.

Bake for 5 minutes. Remove from oven. Cool pie shell in the pan on a wire rack.

EVERGLADE BANANAS

6 TO 8 SERVINGS

6 medium bananas
2 cups dark Jamaican rum
1 cup chopped walnuts
⅓ cup packed light brown sugar
¼ teaspoon ground cinnamon
Dash of freshly grated nutmeg
2 tablespoons unsalted butter, softened
Vanilla ice cream, for serving

Peel bananas and slice crosswise into thirds. Slice each piece of banana lengthwise in half; place in medium bowl. Add rum; cover and set aside to marinate for 30 minutes.

Preheat oven to 400 degrees.

Drain bananas, reserving marinade for another use. Arrange bananas, in a single layer, in lightly greased 13 × 9-inch baking dish.

In small bowl, combine nuts, sugar, cinnamon and nutmeg. With fork, cut butter into sugar mixture until well blended. Sprinkle over bananas.

Bake until bubbly, about 8 minutes.

Turn oven to broil and broil 5 to 6 inches from heat until lightly browned, 1 to 2 minutes.

To serve, spoon warm bananas over vanilla ice cream.

NEW ENGLAND

RECIPES

If any region can lay claim to being the birthplace of American cooking, it is New England. There, at Plymouth Colony, the first Thanksgiving was held in the autumn of 1621. It was a celebration of sheer survival, and it featured, in unaccustomed abundance, the fish, fowl, game, fruits, nuts, and vegetables of the new land. From the sea there were oysters and eels; from the forests, venison and wild goose; and from the land, leeks and watercress, berries and plums. Corn bread was baked, and sweet wine was poured. The grateful Pilgrims shared their feast with Chief Massasiot and his Wampanoag tribe. The Indians, for their part, contributed much of the food and its preparation, and introduced the Pilgrims to the pleasures of popcorn.

The early colonists delighted in such simple treats, particularly the wild fruits and berries of New England. Strawberries, raspberries, blueberries, blackberries, and rarer treasures such as bilberries, treacleberries, and hurtleberries were seasonal favorites. Often the Pilgrims would bake them into pies, tarts, and delicious puddings known variously as grunts, slumps, and flummeries. The newly discovered cranberry, too sour to be enjoyed on its own, was made into jellies and relishes and was thus married to boiled or spit-roasted meats.

Though the hard, rocky soil would grow little except corn, squash, and beans, colonial cooks showed immense inventiveness in preparing these crops. Corn was dried and roasted into samp, ground into hominy, boiled into succotash, and otherwise cooked into johnnycake, mush, pone, spoon bread, and Indian pudding (or a later variation, hasty pudding). This

pudding served both as main course and dessert, depending on how the cornmeal mush was combined with milk, butter, molasses, and spices. Squash, particularly pumpkins, lent themselves to soups, stews, puddings, pies, and even a crude kind of beer. Beans were slow-baked with salt pork, onions, and maple syrup. Cooked on Saturday and consumed on Sunday, when the Puritans forbade any cooking, they became so popular that they eventually gave Boston its famous nickname, "Beantown."

Earlier, regional food had christened an entire peninsula. In 1602, while sailing the waters south of Nova

PRECEDING OVERLEAF: Every autumn, New Hampshire is ablaze with the reds and golds of its spectacular fall foliage.

ABOVE: Plodding through the glistening Vermont snow with a cargo of the state's famed maple syrup.

Scotia, British explorer Bartholomew Gosnold was so bedazzled by the bountiful harvest of fish he found that he dubbed the long promontory curving out into the ocean Cape Cod. And indeed it was cod—fresh, boiled, broiled, fried, dried, salted, pickled, packed, and traded around the globe—that fed the colonists, fertilized their corn, and gave rise to the New England fishing industry.

As if to compensate for the barrenness of the New

England soil and the harshness of the long winters, the sea provided food in abundance. The fresh and salt waters yielded up astonishing wealth. There were salmon and shad, sturgeon, bluefish, and trout from the rivers; clams and oysters, mussels, scallops, and fat, luscious lobsters from the shore; and herring, cod, haddock, smelt, flounder, mackerel, and halibut from the sea. Today, when we indulge in butter-smothered Maine lobster, or warm up on a cold winter's day with a

Lobster traps are neatly stacked on a dock on Mount Desert Island, Maine.

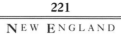
bowl of hot, creamy chowder, we are reaching back centuries to re-create the pleasures of foods well known and loved by our forebears.

As far back as the late eighteenth century, Martha Washington, reacting to the taste of the times for European cuisine, urged women to rediscover the "forgotten" recipes of colonial housewives. Perhaps in response, Amelia Simmons published her forty-seven-page *American Cookery* in Hartford, Connecticut, in 1796. This was the first cookbook written by an American about American cooking, and it was dedicated to the hearty, homespun dishes of the New England farmer. Its success opened the doors for others exploring this distinctive American cuisine. Within a century, Fannie Farmer published *The Boston Cooking School Cook-Book*. Farmer combined a genuine love of French *haute cuisine* with a typically American "scientific" approach to home economics, and thereby thoroughly

A Colonial house in Deerfield, Massachusetts. New England clam chowder is as much a part of our national heritage as this distinctive architecture.

revolutionized the American kitchen.

Today New England cooks are in the midst of still another revolution, intent on conversing with the past while exploring new directions for the future. More than 350 years of experimentation have produced a rich tradition to be borrowed from and built on. The recipes of the early colonists, so closely tied to the land, the sea, and the dishes of northern Europe, have been modified by successive waves of immigrants from Italy, Portugal, Greece, and the Baltic countries. Open hearth cooking, which placed a premium on slow baking, simmering, and spit-roasting—time-consuming methods that are impractical today—has given way to the precisely regulated modern kitchen. And yet, in their love for fresh, locally grown produce, their choice of organic meats and free-range poultry, and their re-kindled passion for seafood, modern cooks are returning to the tastes of their ancestors.

Increasingly, New England inns with working country kitchens turn to local suppliers for *crème fraîche*, butter and cheeses, homemade sausages, vine-ripened berries, and fresh-from-the-garden herbs and spices. Dealing with the earth and its products has assumed its old importance, but as a matter of preference rather than necessity. The old way is often the flavorful way, and, like a forgotten language, it's being rediscovered and spoken once again.

Exotic spices became an integral part of New England home cooking more than three centuries ago, when cargo ships began to arrive laden with ginger, peppercorns, curry, cinnamon bark, and cloves. In the old days they lent strong flavors to an otherwise simple, repetitive cuisine, and masked meats that were sometimes less than perfectly fresh. Today spices enhance

TOP: The early colonists found cranberries in abundance when they arrived in Massachusetts. Here, the berries are harvested by a Nantucket farmer.

ABOVE: Early New Englanders perfected the arts of canning and preserving foods to sustain them through their harsh winters.

rather than hide flavors. Blended in new and subtle combinations, they can literally transform a traditional dish into something sensational. Consider, for example, Boston baked beans with maple and rosemary; or buttery quahog chowder garnished with dill; or trout stuffed with sausage bread, pine nuts, and raisins, then delicately seasoned with nutmeg.

In addition, the rich, caloric sauces of the past are being modified and lightened. Handfuls of fresh herbs, garlic, and other spices lend intensified flavors in a more healthful context. Vegetables, lightly steamed or sautéed, rather than boiled or stewed, are being combined with an eye for bright colors and complementary textures.

For contemporary New England cooks, the juxtaposition of tradition and current fashion poses a new set of challenges. These chefs take pleasure in achieving the broadest possible range of textures, flavors, and colors on the plate. Theirs is the art of presenting meals that are pleasing to the eye, inviting to the palate, and still true to the homespun, stick-to-the-ribs heritage of New England.

LEFT: A fisherman hauls in his catch on the north shore of Massachusetts. New England has always depended heavily on the sea for its cuisine.
RIGHT: A colorful assortment of lobster-trap buoys lines a weathered, shingled wall on the Maine coast.
OVERLEAF: East Orange, Vermont—only one of New England's picture-book villages.

NEW ENGLAND CLAM CHOWDER

Recommended Wine: Sauvignon Blanc

6 SERVINGS

3   dozen steamer clams, in the shell, well
      scrubbed
2   medium potatoes, pared and cut into
      ½-inch cubes
¼   pound sliced bacon, diced
1   small onion, chopped
2   tablespoons all-purpose flour
½   teaspoon salt
1   pint half-and-half, warmed
½   to ¾ teaspoon freshly ground black
      pepper
4   tablespoons unsalted butter
      Chopped fresh dill, optional

Place scrubbed clams in large saucepan. Add 2 cups water, cover and steam over high heat until shells open, about 5 minutes. Remove clams with slotted spoon and set aside. Strain broth through cheesecloth-lined strainer or colander and return broth to pan.

Simmer, uncovered, for 15 minutes. Add potatoes to clam broth and continue to simmer until potatoes are tender and broth is reduced to 1½ cups, 10 to 15 minutes. Remove clam meat from shells; chop and set aside.

In large saucepan, fry bacon over medium heat, stirring frequently, until crisp, 5 to 7 minutes. Remove from pan with slotted spoon and set aside. Discard all but 2 tablespoons bacon drippings. Add onion to drippings and sauté, stirring frequently, until soft, about 5 minutes. Stir in flour and salt and cook, stirring constantly, for 3 minutes. Reduce heat to low and gradually whisk in half-and-half. Stir in clam broth mixture and simmer, stirring frequently, until thickened and bubbly, 8 to 10 minutes.

Add reserved bacon, clams, pepper and 2 tablespoons butter; gently heat through until butter melts. Serve hot, garnished with dill and the remaining 2 tablespoons butter.

BAKING POWDER BISCUITS

MAKES 8 BISCUITS

2½   cups all-purpose flour
1   tablespoon baking powder
¾   teaspoon caraway seeds
½   teaspoon salt

¾   cup half-and-half
4   tablespoons unsalted butter, melted
1   egg yolk, lightly beaten

Piping hot New England Clam Chowder and Baking Powder Biscuits—a time-tested regional remedy for a cold winter's day.

Preheat oven to 400 degrees.

In large mixing bowl, combine flour, baking powder, caraway seeds and salt. Stir in half-and-half, butter and egg yolk, mixing just until dry ingredients are moistened.

Turn dough onto lightly floured surface and knead gently for 1 to 2 minutes. Roll out to 9-inch circle and transfer to lightly greased 9-inch round cake pan. Score top with knife into 8 equal wedges.

Bake until top is lightly browned, 20 to 25 minutes. Serve hot.

BROILED OYSTERS ON THE HALF SHELL

Recommended Wine: Sparkling Wine
6 APPETIZER SERVINGS

2   *cups fresh bread crumbs*
3   *cloves garlic, minced*
6   *tablespoons unsalted butter, melted*
2   *cups loosely packed fresh watercress,*
        finely chopped
2   *dozen oysters on the half shell*
¼   *cup grated Parmesan or Asiago cheese*
        Salt
        Freshly ground pepper
        Lemon wedges, optional

Preheat broiler.

In medium bowl, combine bread crumbs, garlic, butter and watercress; toss to mix well. Spoon mixture evenly over oysters in shell. Top each with ½ teaspoon cheese and a dash of salt and pepper.

Broil 4 to 5 inches from heat until lightly browned, 3 to 5 minutes. Serve with lemon wedges, if desired.

BOSTON BROWN BREAD

MAKES 4 LOAVES

1   *cup yellow cornmeal*
⅔   *cup graham or whole wheat flour*
⅔   *cup rye flour*
⅔   *cup plus 1 tablespoon all-purpose flour*
1   *teaspoon baking soda*
¾   *teaspoon salt*

1   *cup molasses*
2   *eggs, lightly beaten*
1½   *cups buttermilk*
2   *tablespoons brandy*
3   *tablespoons unsalted butter, melted*
1   *cup dried currants*

Put a kettle of water on to boil.

In large mixing bowl, stir together cornmeal, graham and rye flours, ⅔ cup of the all-purpose flour, baking soda and salt; set aside.

In another bowl, blend molasses, eggs, buttermilk and brandy. Add to flour mixture, along with butter and stir until well blended. Toss currants with remaining 1 tablespoon flour and stir into mixture.

Divide batter among 4 well-greased 16-ounce vegetable cans that have been opened at only one end. Cover open end of cans with foil and secure with string. Place a rack in large 6-quart Dutch oven and stand cans on rack. Pour boiling water into Dutch oven to reach 1 inch up the sides of the cans. Bring water back to a boil and reduce heat to low. Cover and simmer for 1¾ to 2 hours, adding more boiling water as needed. Bread will be firm when done.

Remove cans from pan; let stand 10 minutes. Remove bread from cans and serve warm.

Boston Brown Bread with Fresh Cranberry Salad—a perfect New England lunch.

FRESH CRANBERRY SALAD

6 TO 8 SERVINGS

2   *oranges*
2   *Granny Smith apples, cored and*
     chopped
³⁄₄ *pound fresh cranberries, chopped*
²⁄₃ *cup sugar*
2   *cups chopped walnuts*

Peel, seed and dice one orange.

Finely chop remaining orange including peel. In a glass or non-metal bowl, combine oranges with chopped apple, cranberries and sugar. Cover and refrigerate overnight to blend flavors.

Before serving, stir in walnuts.

CARROTS IN MAPLE-DILL SAUCE

6 SERVINGS

¹⁄₂ *cup unsalted butter*
¹⁄₂ *cup pure maple syrup*
3   *pounds carrots, pared and cut into bite-*
     size pieces
1   *to 2 tablespoons chopped fresh dill*

In small saucepan, melt butter with syrup over medium heat, just until mixture begins to boil, about 5 minutes.

Meanwhile, place carrots in steamer basket over boiling water in a 3-quart saucepan. Cover; reduce heat to low. Steam until carrots are crisp-tender, about 7 minutes. Drain and transfer to large serving bowl.

Pour maple syrup mixture over carrots. Add dill and toss gently. Serve immediately.

BOSTON BAKED BEANS

10 TO 12 SERVINGS

2   *pounds dried small white beans, such as*
     pea or navy
1   *large onion*
6   *whole cloves*
¹⁄₄ *pound salt pork, cut into 1-inch pieces*
1   *cup molasses*

¹⁄₄ *cup packed dark brown sugar*
1   *tablespoon dry mustard*
¹⁄₄ *teaspoon ground ginger*
¹⁄₈ *teaspoon freshly ground pepper*

Wash and pick over beans; drain. In 5-

quart Dutch oven, bring 3 quarts water and beans to a boil over high heat. Boil for 2 minutes.

Remove from heat, cover and let beans soak for 30 minutes.

Preheat oven to 300 degrees.

Drain beans, discard liquid and return beans to Dutch oven.

Stud onion with cloves. Add to beans along with 3 quarts water, salt pork, molasses, brown sugar, mustard, ginger and pepper.

Cover and bake until beans are tender, about 6 hours. Add more water, if needed, to keep beans moist.

Before serving, discard clove-studded onion. Serve hot.

ABOVE: The ingredients for Carrots in Maple-Dill Sauce reflect the simplicity of traditional New England cooking.
OVERLEAF: Onions Mornay—a delicately seasoned, stick-to-the-ribs New England delight.

ONIONS MORNAY

6 SERVINGS

2   pounds small white onions, trimmed
4   tablespoons unsalted butter
½   teaspoon dried rosemary, crumbled
¼   teaspoon salt
¼   teaspoon freshly ground pepper
⅛   teaspoon paprika
¼   cup all-purpose flour
2   cups milk, warmed
1   egg, lightly beaten
2   cups shredded Gruyère cheese (about 8
          ounces)
1   cup loosely packed parsley, chopped
2   small cloves garlic, crushed through a
          press
½   cup fine dry bread crumbs

Preheat oven to 375 degrees.

In large saucepan, steam onions over boiling water until just tender, 10 to 15 minutes. Drain and place in lightly buttered 2-quart baking dish; set aside.

In medium saucepan, melt butter over medium heat; add rosemary, salt, pepper and paprika. Stir in flour and cook, stirring constantly, for 3 minutes. Reduce heat to low and gradually whisk in warm milk. Cook and stir until thickened and bubbly, about 5 minutes.

Place egg in small bowl. Add ½ cup of hot milk mixture to beaten egg and blend to warm egg. Stir egg mixture into milk mixture. Add all but 3 tablespoons cheese, stirring constantly, until melted, about 3 minutes. Remove from heat and pour over onions in baking dish; toss gently.

In small bowl, combine remaining 3 tablespoons cheese, parsley, garlic and bread crumbs. Sprinkle over onions and cheese sauce. Bake until bubbly and lightly browned, 15 to 20 minutes.

BOILED LOBSTER

Recommended Wine: Chardonnay

Bring enough water to cover lobsters to a boil in very large covered pot. Add 1 teaspoon salt for every quart of water. Plunge lobsters head first into boiling water. Bring water back to a boil and reduce heat to low. Cover and cook 1-pound lobsters for 7 minutes and 2-pound lobsters for 10 minutes.

Remove lobsters with tongs and plunge into cold water for a few seconds to stop the cooking.

To serve, cut off claws and crack open with nutcracker. Cut through head and remove small sac (stomach) and intestinal vein. Place lobster on its back and cut lengthwise from where tail and body meet down to the tail, for easy serving. With a small fork ease tail meat from shell. Serve with warm drawn butter.

BREADED STEAMER CLAMS

Recommended Wine: Johannisberg Riesling

6 SERVINGS

6   dozen steamer clams, scrubbed
1   cup all-purpose flour
1   teaspoon paprika
1   clove garlic, minced
2   tablespoons finely chopped onion
¼   teaspoon freshly ground white pepper
1   egg, lightly beaten
½   cup milk
1   cup fine dry bread crumbs
½   cup unsalted butter
¾   cup vegetable oil
    Tartar Sauce (recipe follows)

Shuck and drain clams; set aside.

In shallow plate combine flour, paprika, garlic, onion and pepper; set aside. In shallow bowl, mix egg with milk; set aside. Pour bread crumbs onto a third plate.

Dredge each clam in flour mixture, shaking off excess. Dip flour coated clam in egg mixture, then roll in bread crumbs until completely coated. Place coated clams on baking sheet; repeat with remaining clams.

In large, heavy skillet, melt butter with oil over high heat. Fry clams, 6 to 8 at a time, until richly browned, 15 to 20 seconds on each side. Transfer with slotted spoon to paper towels; drain and keep warm. Serve with Tartar Sauce.

TARTAR SAUCE

MAKES 1½ CUPS

1   cup mayonnaise
1   small dill pickle, minced
1   scallion, minced
2   tablespoons minced celery
3   tablespoons minced fresh parsley
1   tablespoon capers, minced
1   clove garlic, crushed through a press
1   tablespoon fresh lemon juice
½   teaspoon Worcestershire sauce
1   drop hot pepper sauce

Mix ingredients together in small bowl. Cover and refrigerate until chilled to blend flavors, at least 30 minutes.

PRECEDING OVERLEAF: Boiled Lobster—the cornerstone of Maine's cuisine.

COD FISH AND CHIPS

Recommended Wine: Fumé Blanc

6 SERVINGS

8   *medium-size white potatoes, pared*
2   *to 3 quarts vegetable oil*
3   *pounds fresh cod fish fillets*
1½ *cups all-purpose flour*
½   *teaspoon salt*
¼   *teaspoon freshly ground pepper*
2   *eggs, lightly beaten*
1½ *cups milk*
1   *teaspoon dried thyme*
    Additional salt and lemon wedges, for
      serving

Cut potatoes into ¼-inch slices. Cut slices lengthwise into ¼-inch strips. Place potatoes in large bowl and add ice water to cover; set aside.

Preheat oven to 200 degrees.

In 5-quart Dutch oven or electric skillet over medium high heat, heat about 2-inches oil to 375 degrees on deep fat thermometer.

Meanwhile, rinse fish under cold running water and pat dry with paper towels.

In shallow dish or plate, combine flour, salt and pepper.

In medium bowl, beat together eggs, milk and thyme.

Using tongs, coat fish with egg mixture then roll in flour mixture, turning to coat all sides. Coat fish a second time in egg and then flour mixture. Repeat with remaining fish.

Place fish on wire rack; set aside.

Drain potatoes; pat completely dry with paper towels.

Fry potatoes in a single layer in hot oil until golden brown, about 5 minutes. Drain on paper towels. Place potatoes on ovenproof platter and keep warm in oven while cooking remaining potatoes and fish.

Add more oil, if necessary, to maintain a depth of 2 inches. Let oil heat to 375 degrees.

When hot, fry fish fillets, a few at a time, turning once until golden, 5 to 7 minutes. Drain on paper towels. Repeat with remaining fish.

To serve, season potatoes to taste with salt. Garnish fish with lemon wedges.

BAKED FISH WITH OYSTER DRESSING

Recommended Wine: Chardonnay

8 SERVINGS

1	*whole bass, bluefish, cod or haddock (3½ to 4½ pounds), dressed*
1	*lemon, thinly sliced*
¼	*teaspoon salt*
⅛	*teaspoon freshly ground pepper*
1½	*cups coarse cracker crumbs*
½	*teaspoon dried basil, crumbled*
¼	*teaspoon dried thyme, crumbled*
⅛	*teaspoon dried rosemary, crumbled*
¼	*cup finely chopped fresh parsley*
1	*medium onion, chopped*
2	*cloves garlic, minced*
1	*rib celery, chopped*
8	*tablespoons unsalted butter*
½	*pint (8 ounces) shucked oysters, drained and coarsely chopped*
1	*teaspoon grated lemon zest*

Preheat oven to 375 degrees.

Rinse fish under cold running water; pat dry with paper towels. Lightly grease a jelly roll pan. Arrange lemon slices in center of pan and place fish on top. Sprinkle cavity of fish with salt and pepper and leave open.

In medium bowl, combine cracker crumbs, basil, thyme, rosemary and parsley; set aside.

In small skillet, sauté onion, garlic and celery in 4 tablespoons butter over medium heat until onion just begins to brown, 8 to 10 minutes. Remove from heat. Add oysters, lemon zest and cracker mixture, toss gently.

Stuff one side of fish cavity with oyster mixture and close fish.

Melt 3 tablespoons butter. Brush fish with butter. Bake for 10 minutes per inch of thickness (measured at thickest part), or until fish flakes easily at backbone. Baste fish occasionally with remaining tablespoon melted butter.

Transfer fish to serving platter. Pull out fins. Remove upper fillet from backbone by cutting down center back of cooked fish to backbone and ribs. Remove and discard backbone and ribs. Cut fillets to serve. Spoon dressing into serving bowl.

NEW ENGLAND CORNED BEEF AND BABY VEGETABLE BOILED DINNER

Recommended Wine: Pinot Noir

SERVES 6 TO 8

4   to 5 pound corned beef brisket
2   bay leaves
12   whole black peppercorns
1   small cinnamon stick
3   whole allspice berries
2   whole cloves
1½   teaspoons mustard seed
4   cloves garlic, sliced
16   small red new potatoes
2   turnips or parsnips, pared and
       quartered
16   small white onions
2   bunches baby carrots, pared including
       ½-inch of the green tops
3   cups Brussels sprouts, trimmed
     Brandy Brisket Glaze (recipe follows)
     Mustard Sauce (recipe follows)

Rinse brisket and place in 5-quart Dutch oven. Add enough water to cover meat. Add bay leaves, peppercorns, cinnamon stick, allspice, cloves, mustard seed and garlic. Bring to a boil over high heat. Reduce heat to low, cover and simmer until brisket is tender, 2½ to 3 hours.

Preheat oven to 375 degrees.

Transfer brisket and 1 cup of the cooking liquid to a large baking pan; set aside.

Bring the remaining cooking liquid to a boil over medium-high heat and add potatoes and turnips; reduce heat to medium and simmer 10 minutes. Add onions and simmer 5 minutes. Add carrots and Brussels sprouts and simmer until vegetables are tender, 5 to 10 minutes.

While vegetables are cooking, drizzle one-third of Brandy Brisket Glaze over brisket in pan. Bake until richly browned, 15 to 20 minutes, basting frequently with remaining glaze mixture.

Slice and arrange brisket on heated serving platter. Transfer vegetables to serving platter with slotted spoon. Pass Mustard Sauce.

BRANDY BRISKET GLAZE

MAKES 1 CUP

1   6-ounce can frozen apple juice
        concentrate, thawed
½   cup firmly packed dark brown sugar
1   tablespoon dry mustard
¼   cup brandy

In small saucepan, combine apple juice, brown sugar and mustard. Cook over medium heat, stirring frequently, until mixture thickens and boils, about 10 minutes. Remove from heat and stir in brandy.

ABOVE AND OPPOSITE: The classic New England boiled dinner is given a tangy updating with Brandy Brisket Glaze and Mustard Sauce for the vegetables.

MUSTARD SAUCE FOR BOILED VEGETABLES

MAKES 2½ CUPS

2   tablespoons unsalted butter
1   medium onion, finely chopped
3   tablespoons all-purpose flour
1   teaspoon salt
1   tablespoon dry mustard
¼   teaspoon freshly ground white pepper
2   cups milk, warmed
1   to 2 teaspoons freshly grated horseradish

In medium saucepan, melt butter over medium heat. Add onion and cook, stirring frequently, until soft, about 5 minutes. Stir in flour, salt, dry mustard and pepper and cook, stirring constantly, for 3 minutes.

Reduce heat to low and gradually whisk in warm milk. Cook and stir until thickened and bubbly, 3 to 5 minutes. Remove from heat and stir in horseradish. Serve with boiled vegetables.

BOSTON CREAM PIE

MAKES 1 CAKE

CAKE

2   cups cake flour
2   teaspoons baking powder
1/8 teaspoon salt
2/3 cup unsalted butter, at room
        temperature
1 1/3 cups granulated sugar
1   teaspoon vanilla extract
2/3 cup milk
4   egg whites, at room temperature
1/4 cup raspberry jam

CUSTARD FILLING

1/2 vanilla bean
1   cup milk
2   tablespoons all-purpose flour
1/3 cup granulated sugar
1   egg, lightly beaten
2   egg yolks, at room temperature

CHOCOLATE GLAZE

1   ounce unsweetened chocolate
2   tablespoons unsalted butter
1   cup powdered sugar, sifted
3   tablespoons heavy cream
     Powdered sugar and fresh fruit, for
        garnish

Make cake: Preheat oven to 350 degrees.

On sheet of waxed paper, sift together cake flour, baking powder and salt; set aside.

In large mixing bowl, beat butter, sugar and vanilla at high speed until light and fluffy. Add dry ingredients alternately with the milk, beating well after each addition.

In large mixing bowl, beat egg whites at high speed until stiff but not dry. Gently fold whites into flour mixture.

Turn batter into 2 greased and floured 9-inch round baking pans. Bake until a cake tester inserted in the center comes out clean, 25 to 30 minutes.

Cool cakes in pans on wire rack for 10 minutes. Remove cakes from pans and let cool completely on wire rack.

Meanwhile, make custard filling: Split vanilla bean lengthwise and scrape out the tiny black seeds.

In small saucepan, combine pod and seeds with milk. Place over medium-high heat until milk just begins to boil. Remove vanilla bean pod.

In small bowl, combine all-purpose flour and sugar. Stir in egg and egg yolks. Gradually whisk hot milk into egg mixture. Return pan to heat and cook over medium-low heat, stirring constantly, until custard bubbles and thickens, about 5 minutes.

Pour into small bowl; cover with

PRECEDING OVERLEAF: Boston Cream Pie is always a satisfying conclusion to a special dinner.

plastic wrap placed directly on surface of custard. Chill for about 2 hours before assembling cake.

Make chocolate glaze: In small saucepan, melt chocolate with butter over low heat. Off heat, stir in powdered sugar and cream until smooth.

Assemble cake: Place one cake layer on serving plate. Spread with all of raspberry jam. Spoon chilled Custard Filling over jam layer. Top with second cake layer. Pour Chocolate Glaze on top of cake and gently spread out to edges. Refrigerate until chilled, about 1 hour. Garnish with sifted powdered sugar and fresh fruit before serving.

BLUEBERRY SLUMP

Recommended Wine: White Riesling
8 SERVINGS

2 pounds fresh blueberries
  Juice of 1 lemon
½ cup plus 2 tablespoons sugar
2 tablespoons cornstarch
¾ teaspoon ground cinnamon
¼ teaspoon ground cardamom
1½ cups all-purpose flour
1 teaspoon baking powder
⅛ teaspoon salt
⅛ teaspoon freshly grated nutmeg
⅛ teaspoon ground ginger
⅛ teaspoon ground mace
1 teaspoon finely grated lemon zest
6 tablespoons unsalted butter, chilled
⅔ cup milk
  Crème fraîche (recipe follows)

Preheat oven to 425 degrees.

In large glass or non-metal bowl, combine blueberries, lemon juice, ½ cup sugar, cornstarch, cinnamon and cardamom. Divide mixture evenly among 8 lightly greased 10- or 12-ounce baking dishes.

In medium bowl, combine flour, remaining 2 tablespoons sugar, baking powder, salt, nutmeg, ginger, mace and lemon zest. Cut in butter with pastry blender or 2 knives until mixture resembles coarse crumbs. Add milk and stir just until dry ingredients are moistened.

Divide dough into 8 equal parts and drop by spoonfuls onto blueberry mixture.

Bake until berries are bubbly and top is golden, 30 to 35 minutes. Serve with crème fraîche.

CREME FRAICHE

MAKES 2 CUPS

2   cups heavy cream
1   tablespoon buttermilk

In small saucepan over low heat, warm cream slightly (95 degrees).

Pour into a glass or non-metal bowl.

Stir in buttermilk and cover loosely with plastic wrap. Let stand at room temperature until thickened, 12 to 24 hours.

Refrigerate, covered, for up to 2 weeks.

RASPBERRY SANDWICH TEA COOKIES

Recommended Wine: Muscat Canelli

MAKES 2½ DOZEN

2½ cups all-purpose flour
2   teaspoons baking powder
½   cup unsalted butter
1¾ cups sugar
1   teaspoon lemon extract
2   eggs, lightly beaten
2   cups fresh or frozen red raspberries
½   cup applesauce
2   teaspoons fresh lemon juice

In small bowl, combine flour and baking powder; set aside.

In large mixing bowl, cream butter, ½ cup sugar and lemon extract with electric mixer at medium speed.

Add eggs and beat until smooth. Gradually blend flour mixture into creamed mixture. Beat at high speed for 2 minutes, scraping down bowl twice.

Divide dough in half and shape into 2 balls. Wrap separately in plastic wrap and refrigerate until chilled, about 3 hours.

Meanwhile, prepare raspberry mixture: In small saucepan over high heat, bring remaining 1¼ cups sugar, berries, applesauce and lemon juice to a boil, stirring constantly.

Reduce heat to medium and cook, stirring constantly, until mixture will not move when dropped on a plate, 15 to 20 minutes.

Cover and refrigerate until chilled, about 30 minutes.

Preheat oven to 375 degrees. Lightly grease 2 or more baking sheets.

Roll out one portion of dough on

lightly floured surface about ¼ inch thick.

Using floured 2½-inch cookie cutter or rim of glass, cut out 30 circles of dough. Add scraps to remaining portion of dough and roll out. Cut out 30 more circles of dough, using dough scraps if necessary to produce a total of 60 circles.

Using a 1-inch round cookie cutter, cut out centers from 30 rounds.

Place solid and cut-out rounds on prepared baking sheets and bake until lightly browned, 8 to 10 minutes. Cool on wire racks.

When cool, spread about 2 teaspoonfuls of raspberry mixture over bottom of each solid cookie.

Top with a cut-out cookie, browned side up, to make a sandwich. Repeat with remaining cookies and raspberry mixture to make a total of 30 cookies.

CREDITS

Photo Credits

page 195 © Jose Fernandez/Woodfin Camp & Associates

pages 217–218 © Craig Aurness/Wooodfin Camp & Associates

page 219 © Nathan Benn/Woodfin Camp & Associates

page 220 © Robert Frerck/Woodfin Camp & Associates

page 221 © Craig Aurness/Woodfin Camp & Associates

page 222, top © Robert Frerck/Woodfin Camp & Associates

page 222, bottom © Rick Winsor/Woodfin Camp & Associates

page 223, left © Nathan Benn/Woodfin Camp & Associates

page 223, right © Robert Frerck/Woodfin Camp & Associates

pages 224–225 © Chuck O'Rear/Woodfin Camp & Associates

Prop Credits

page 26 Crystal glass courtesy Baccarat, 55 East 57th Street, New York, New York

page 40 Silver fork courtesy James II Galleries, 15 East 57th Street, New York, New York

page 57 Fluted Leeds bowl courtesy James II Galleries, 15 East 57th Street, New York, New York

page 59 Victorian spice set and glass bowl courtesy James II Galleries, 15 East 57th Street, New York, New York

page 63 Hand-blown crystal wine goblets courtesy Simon Pearce, 385 Bleecker Street, New York, New York

pages 88–89 Crystal goblet courtesy Baccarat, 55 East 57th Street, New York, New York

page 94 Hand-blown crystal goblet courtesy Simon Pearce, 385 Bleecker Street, New York, New York

page 106 Hand-blown crystal goblets courtesy Simon Pearce, 385 Bleecker Street, New York, New York

Plate and Patino Wolf flatware courtesy Zona, 97 Greene Street, New York, New York

page 109 Bowls courtesy Zona, 97 Greene Street, New York, New York

page 118 Terra cotta plate and bowl courtesy Zona, 97 Greene Street, New York, New York

page 123 Glass plate courtesy Zona, 97 Greene Street, New York, New York

page 136 Hand-blown crystal pitcher courtesy Simon Pearce, 385 Bleecker, New York, New York

page 137 Crystal wine glasses courtesy Baccarat, 55 East 57th Street, New York, New York
Sterling silver ladel courtesy Buccellati, 46 East 57 Street, New York, New York

page 141 "Cactus" plate courtesy Georg Jensen
Sterling silver fork courtesy Royal Copenhagen, 683 Madison Avenue, New York, New York

page 145 Hand-thrown porcelain platter by Lynn Evans for Gordon Foster, 1322 Third Avenue, New York, New York
Crystal goblets courtesy Baccarat, 55 East 57th Street, New York, New York

Page 185 "St. Remy" crystal wine glasses courtesy Baccarat, 55 East 57th Street, New York, New York

page 201 "Continental" sterling silver fork by Georg Jensen for Royal Copenhagen, 683 Madison Avenue, New York, New York

page 205 Crystal wine glasses courtesy Baccarat, 55 East 57th Street, New York, New York

pages 234–235 Antique Spode platter and glass bowl courtesy James II Galleries, 15 East 57th Street, New York, New York
Hand-blown crystal goblet courtesy Simon Pearce, 385 Bleecker Street, New York, New York

pages 242–243 Antique silver pie server courtesy James II Galleries, 15 East 57th Street, New York, New York

Tables throughout, courtesy Pierre Deux, 367-369 Bleecker Street, New York, New York

Flowers throughout, courtesy Very Special Flowers, 215 West 10th Street, New York, New York

Text Credits

John Doerper researches food and wine of the West with nonstop travels up and down the coast. Specializing in the Northwest, he is a regular contributor to *Washington Magazine* and the *Seattle Times* and has written several books on the abundance of the region.

Paul R. Gregutt has worked as a disc jockey, television reporter, and writer in Seattle. He is a contributor to *The Wine Spectator* and is the wine columnist for Seattle's *The Weekly*. He is currently working on his first play, set in a wine cellar.

Joanne Will is a former food editor of the *Chicago Tribune*. She has always lived in the Midwest, where she experiences heartland food first hand. She currently promotes foods and food products through her work at Hill and Knowlton.

INDEX

Composed in Caslon 540 and Cloister Open Face
by Trufont Typographers, Inc., Hicksville, New York

Printed and bound by Amilcare Pizzi s.p.a.-arti grafiche, Milan, Italy